Clergy Malpractice

Clergy Malpractice

H. Newton Malony
Thomas L. Needham
Samuel Southard

The Westminster Press
Philadelphia

Scripture quotations from the Revised Standard Version of the Bible are copyrighted 1946, 1952, ©1971, 1973 by the Division of Christian Education of the National Council of the Churches of Christ in the U.S.A. and are used by permission.

Grateful acknowledgment is made to the authors and publishers for permission to reprint, in chapter 2, Samuel E. Ericsson's article, "Clergyman Malpractice: Ramifications of a New Theory," from the *Valparaiso University Law Review* 16(1):163–184 (Fall 1981), and Ben Zion Bergman's article, "Is the Cloth Unraveling? A First Look at Clergy Malpractice," from the *San Fernando Valley Law Review* 9:47–66 (1981).

Book design by Gene Harris

First edition

Published by The Westminster Press®
Philadelphia, Pennsylvania

PRINTED IN THE UNITED STATES OF AMERICA

9 8 7 6 5 4 3 2 1

Library of Congress Cataloging-in-Publication Data

Malony, H. Newton
  Clergy malpractice

  Bibliography: p.
  1. Clergy—Malpractice—United States. 2. Pastoral Counseling. I. Needham, Thomas L. II. Southard, Samuel.
KF4868.C44C55 1986   346.7303′3   85-31466
ISBN 0-664-24591-9 (pbk).   347.30633

Contents

Preface

The evaluation of clergy functioning is the new dilemma of our age. Clergy were once held sacrosanct, invulnerable to the legal manipulations of the marketplace. This day has passed if recent experience is any key to the future.

It is our conviction that the issues of good and bad ministerial functioning need to be openly and frankly discussed. Our hope is that these essays will provide insight and provoke dialogue about these important issues.

We want to express our appreciation to several individuals who have provided invaluable assistance in the various tasks and stages of this manuscript.

First, we wish to thank Dr. Jess Moody, Senior Pastor of the First Baptist Church of Van Nuys, California, for encouraging Dr. Needham to conduct a Clergy Malpractice workshop in 1980. Along with Ronald M. Supancic, Attorney-at-Law, and Sam Alexander, President of S. L. Alexander Insurance, Inc., we offered several workshops, which generated substantial and ongoing interest in the newly emerging clergy litigation crisis.

Second, we are thankful to the many individuals who either provided us with or directed us to pertinent information. A note of thanks is due Dr. David Seregow of San Jose, California, for researching court documents in the Santa Clara County Superior Court. We are grateful to Samuel E. Ericsson, National Director of the Christian Legal Society and defense attorney for Rev. John MacArthur in the Grace Community Church suit, for providing us with articles, publications, and a myriad of court documents. We are indebted to the kind interest and assistance provided by several insurance company executives; in lengthy telephone conversations, as well as by providing documents and directions to reference materials, the following have greatly enriched the insurance chapter: Robert Plunk, J.D., Executive Vice-President, Chad Hensley, Chief Executive Officer, and Jack Kelly, Director of Commercial Marketing, all of Preferred Risk Mutual Insurance Company; Al Davidson, Vice-President Claims, David Roth, Assistant Vice-President of Product Development, and Al Leatherman, Vice-President Marketing, of Brotherhood Mutual Insurance Company; and John Cleary, Secretary and General Counsel, Church Mutual Insurance.

Finally, we wish to express heartfelt thanks to each of our secretaries, who provided essential assistance in coordinating and gathering information, typing, editing, and proofreading: Marian Moss, secretary to H. Newton Malony; Jean Hedge, secretary to Thomas L. Needham; and Annette Kakimoto, secretary to Samuel Southhard.

H.N.M.
T.L.N.
S.S

1

Malpractice in the Ministry

Thomas L. Needham

Is the clergy malpractice crisis over? No, it is not over, and this book has been written to help clergy and churches understand the nature of the legal assaults against the way ministry is practiced. In this chapter, seven interrelated dimensions of the problem are introduced. Then, in following chapters, we will discuss how churches can safeguard their insurance coverage and reduce the risk of legal entanglements by reexamining the biblical foundations and practical implications of their philosophies of pastoral care and counseling, whether provided by ministers or laity.

Initially the discussion of clergy malpractice may seem confusing. Most of the opinions expressed in Christian periodicals and by prominent Christian leaders since the May 1985 dismissal of the first clergy malpractice suit have not been put into the context of the overall problem and are therefore misleading and overly optimistic.[1] Such optimism, guarded though it may have been, was nonetheless typically assumed in articles like the one in *The Christian Century:*

> After days of testimony filled with talk of sin and biblical principles, a Los Angeles judge dismissed all charges in the first "clergy malpractice" case—and with that decision probably eased the minds of thousands of ministers.[2]

Samuel Ericsson, defense attorney for Grace Community Church's senior pastor, John F. MacArthur, Jr., and Special Counsel, Center for Law and Religious Freedom of the Christian Legal Society in Washington, D.C., expressed unqualified optimism over the dismissal.

> It closes the door to any future suits seeking to make pastoral
> counseling accountable to the state . . . and it prevents a legal
> wedge from being placed between those who need help most and
> those who stand most ready to help.[3]

Why, then, is there still a malpractice crisis? How is it that
such commonly held optimism can be misleading without a
broader perspective of the Grace Church suit? And why are
such issues as the legal mood of the American public and the
nature of current ecclesiastical litigation important considerations? We will answer these questions by examining seven aspects of the problem: (1) consumer protection, (2) contemporary attitudes toward professionals, (3) the professional
malpractice crisis, (4) the clash of conservatives with psychology, (5) the probable first clergy malpractice case, (6) *Nally v.
Grace Community Church of the Valley,* and (7) the church as
defendant: pending litigation.

Consumer Protection

The term consumer protection, according to University of
Illinois professor Laurence Feldman, suggests that consumers
need to be protected against sellers who are either ignorant of
certain realities in the marketplace or who deliberately attempt
to defraud the consumer.[4] It is a movement that demonstrates
the profound impact that public sentiment can have upon individuals and corporations. Why did it develop?

Consumer protection developed out of the increasing industrialization and urbanization of post–Civil War America. No
longer were food products produced locally, where quality was
assured and consumer satisfaction was an integral part of the
future of the store. "It was an age of production in a sellers'
market, and all kinds of fraudulent, shoddy, adulterated, and
dangerous products were pumped into the marketplace,
[thereby making] the existing framework of seller-consumption
relationships obsolete" (Feldman, p. 4).

From this first era (1860s to World War I), which yielded the
first federal regulations in 1874, the first U.S. Senate investigations in 1899, and food and drug control in 1906, emerged a
movement based on the belief that "there were many consumers who were incapable of directly appraising the inherent at-
tributes of the products they were ingesting" (p. 7).

During the Depression, consumer protectionism strengthened in this second period (1927 to World War II) because a strong antibusiness attitude developed. Many people blamed the economic crisis on "big business." Books such as Upton Sinclair's *The Jungle* were central in initiating and perpetuating this era: "The public indignation generated by these books crystallized in the efforts of several pro-consumer lobbying groups and was translated into legislative action" (Feldman, p. 9).

Consumer concerns in the contemporary period (1960 to the present), with Ralph Nader as a prominent spokesperson, expanded from food and drug regulation to automobile safety, product advertising and marketing, and problems of children and the elderly. This period saw the idea of consumer protection accepted by both the executive and the legislative branches of the federal government. The sixties saw John F. Kennedy's "consumer bill of rights"; and his successor, Lyndon Baines Johnson, created the White House post of Special Assistant for Consumer Affairs. There was more protective legislation passed in the seventies than in the preceding seven decades combined.

The factors that gave rise to this concern for the rights of consumers and the need to protect them against what are perceived to be unfair practices are important to clergy litigation and malpractice. The three major causes of the solidification of consumer protection, according to Professor Feldman, are the extensive existence of questionable marketing practices, technological complexity and repair problems, and better educated and more affluent consumers.[5] These same factors also affect public attitudes toward the consumer as a client in the professional-client relationship.

Contemporary Attitudes Toward Professionals

Professionals—such as doctors, accountants, lawyers, and psychologists—enjoy prestige and acceptance by the American public. How have they fared up against the public mood of wanting to be protected?

Duke Divinity School ethicist Dennis Campbell writes that professionals have become increasingly vulnerable to their clients, many of whom, with a higher level of general education, are now questioning both their competence and their dedication. Physicians were the initial focus of these questions.

Malpractice suits have escalated dramatically in the past two decades. The reasons are manifold and have to do with the desire of attorneys to accept the cases, the willingness of members of the medical profession to criticize colleagues; but the underlying reason is that the American public is not willing to accept unquestionably the claims of competence on the part of physicians.[6]

How can the dedication and competence of individuals with seven to ten years of educational training be in question? Campbell contends that their primary vulnerability results from a two-fold failure in the professional education process—failure to develop moral character and to provide training in how to make moral decisions. By reviewing the definition of a professional, one can quickly see why inadequate and ethically neutral training creates a crisis. Campbell (pp. 21–25) defines a professional as one:

Who is engaged in a social service that is essential and unique

Who has developed a high degree of knowledge

Who must develop the ability to apply the special body of knowledge that is unique to the profession

Who is part of a group that is autonomous and claims the right to regulate itself

Who recognizes and affirms a code of ethics

Who exhibits a strong self-discipline and accepts personal responsibility for actions and decisions

Whose primary concern and commitment is to communal interest rather than merely to the self

Who is more concerned with services rendered than with financial rewards

With the high degree of trust society has placed in professionals, who function primarily in an autonomous manner, why is it that the educational institutions in which they are trained promote ethical neutrality? While the answer is multifaceted, the main reason is the secularization of American life and values to accommodate the rights and needs of a religiously pluralistic society. As ethicist Campbell succinctly describes, the loss of Christian foundations is at the heart of religious pluralism and secularization so that "official and public conceptions of common life are not fundamentally informed by a theological vision" (p. 31). Subsequently, given their largely autonomous functioning, limited moral development, and inadequate decision-making skills, professionals are left to make judgments based upon highly subjective and frequently self-serving moral ideals.

Many churches and religious leaders, both liberal and conservative, propose solutions based on their unique assessment of the underlying moral crisis. We will discuss the risk involved in some of the proposed solutions after we look more closely at the legal predicament that public discontent and ethical neutrality have brought to the professional community.

The Professional Malpractice Crisis

The concept of malpractice has expanded to all professions and is finding wider and wider applications within each one. According to *Black's Law Dictionary,* malpractice is a lack of skill or failure to perform up to standard in professional practice. Black also includes illegal or immoral conduct in his definition.[7]

Originally, malpractice was applied primarily to physicians, reaching what was considered crisis proportions in the mid-seventies. That was not the worst, however; during the last ten years malpractice claims have tripled and the losses to insurance companies have doubled, heaping up annual costs in excess of $2 billion. As a result, for example, one Florida obstetrician paid $52,000 for his 1985 premium, while a New York State neurosurgeon paid $101,000.[8]

Malpractice has recently become of increasing concern to the members of the American Psychological Association (APA). From 1976 to 1981 an average of 44 malpractice suits were filed annually. That situation has radically changed since 1982, with an average of 153 suits now being filed each year. The largest area of increase for malpractice suits has been for sexual misconduct. In the 1976–81 period, sexual misconduct accounted for about 9 percent of the suits filed, while in the later period it accounted for nearly 50 percent.[9]

Dr. Nicholas Cummings, former president of the APA and chair of that organization's insurance trust, cites the size of awards, the lifting of the statute of limitations, and the expanded liability of therapists for professional decisions as resulting from changing public attitudes, the greater sophistication of lawsuits, and new legal interpretations. He reported that in 1984 two claims alone were settled for a combined total of over $3 million.[10]

Where this crisis in therapist responsibility will end is not clear. Cummings described a recent incident in which the courts reinterpreted the three-year statute of limitations as beginning when the emotionally injured person realizes his or her rights rather than when the incident occurred. Subsequently, with an eye toward increased responsibility of the therapist and the lifting of the statute of limitations, a court has agreed to go to trial in a case where "a man who is now a young adult is alleging that his mother received improper psychotherapy from a psychologist when he was five years old, thus giving him a bad childhood."[11]

Both the manner and the extent to which many churches are or easily could become entangled in this kind of consumer protection litigation are quite startling. In order to minimize risks, it is essential to become familiar with both the reasons and the consequences of the clash between Christians and psychology.

The Clash of Conservatives with Psychology

Increasingly, church leaders have developed counseling methods and services to help individuals with their personal problems and moral issues. However, there are strategies to these converging moral and psychological troubles that can generate more problems than they solve. Some of these strategies hasten the logical progression by which consumer protection and the public discontent with autonomously functioning professionals come to be targeted toward clergy and the church. One such strategy is the categorical rejection of psychological knowledge and technique.

This rejection, especially of psychotherapy, is woven into a larger rejection of humanistic and secularized values. While it is true that psychological theory is replete with naturalistic metaphors (such as "organismic self-regulation") that emphasize the ability of persons to heal and guide themselves when provided with a nonjudgmental relationship (moral neutrality), and while it is also true that most Evangelicals and Evangelical institutions, including theological seminaries, have not adequately grasped the critical problem presented by these underlying naturalistic metaphors which are embedded deep within each system of psychotherapy, it does not follow that we should totally abandon psychology. That would be rejecting the good along with the inadequate and potentially harmful. Admittedly, there are no easy short-term solutions. Nonetheless, the consequences of either extreme—unqualified acceptance or unqualified rejection—will lead on the one hand to the diminishing of the cause of Christ and on the other to a high-risk legal vulnerability.

In spite of the need for truly integrative work, perpetuation of the complex unresolved issues of integrating psychology into theology and ministry—specifically the problem of setting priorities for the psychological agendas—most likely will continue to be a predominant factor in the categorical rejection of psychological counseling by certain segments of the Christian community. Since the general public regards such counseling as the norm, those churches and clergy who reject it will remain highly vulnerable to litigation in their lay and pastoral care and counseling ministries to deeply troubled individuals, couples, and families. The resolution will not be easy.

There have been four central historical movements leading to this hazardous polarization: (1) the historical development of Protestant theology, (2) the pastoral counseling movement, (3) the historical development of American psychology, and (4) the institutionalization of the polarization.

The Development of Protestant Theology

Since the Renaissance, theology has developed as an academic study in much the same way as have other university disciplines. As Vanderbilt University professor Edward Farley notes, what was previously the knowledge of God became an abstract and impersonal knowledge.[12] As such, theology is "a discipline, a course of studies, a career and teaching specialty, a necessity for ministry, a Hellenistic-Christian mode of thinking" (Farley, p. 22). Theology faculties are left with a severe problem. Theology has become a scholarly education for clergy rather than a godly reflection on personal-existential life (pp. 25, 27).

A further distancing of theology from daily life came to eighteenth-century American theological thought when seminaries accepted Schleiermacher's distinction between theory (disciplines like Bible, church history, and ethics) and clergy practice (practical theology, preaching, and pastoral care; cf. Farley, p. 28).

As the focus of the practice of theology was reduced to clergy duties, and that further to ministerial technology, it was inevitable that applied or practical theology would be severed from the individual or social aspects of moral life.[13] When the concern for direction in the Christian life turned toward personal faith, it was assumed that the self-sustaining aspects of one's faith were spontaneously known even though the context of life was increasingly pluralistic and socially transitional.[14] It is within this vacuum that pastoral counseling emerged.

The Predicament of "Pastoral" Counseling

As the American psychotherapy disciplines of psychiatry and psychology developed, ministers "incorporated" therapeutic insights into their ministries. All seemed well. However, the alienated plight of practical theology, artificially divorced from theology and ethics, inevitably led to an overidentification of the pastor with secular counseling and psychotherapy. Paul Pruyser, in *The Minister as Diagnostician*, kindly and meticulously focused his own personal concern on pastors trained at the Menninger Clinic. He observed that after receiving counselor training, these pastors became indistinguishable from secular therapists; they lost their spiritual and moral mission. He wrote to help ministers discover how to assist psychiatric patients in developing a relevant faith.[15]

Theologians, too, have long recognized the problem.[16] Don Browning has been one of the foremost of articulate writers to discuss the extent of the impact of secular psychotherapy upon pastoral care and counseling. Browning wrote:

> Sometimes the relation to the social sciences is so prominent in a particular region of practical theology that the region comes close to being identified with that science, such as has been the case in pastoral care's identification with psychotherapy.[17]

In his highly significant volume *The Moral Context of Pastoral Care,* Browning portrayed the moral dilemma of the pastoral counseling movement that had overidentified itself with morally neutral and sometimes counterculture systems of psychotherapy,[18] noting that "the major difference between the minister and the secular psychotherapist is that the minister has a direct professional responsibility to help shape this moral universe of values and meanings."[19]

The Development of American Psychology

The portrayal of this moral dilemma is sharpened when, in reviewing the historical roots of American psychology, one discovers that, like theology, psychology evolved toward an isolated, noninterdisciplinary study. Two hundred years ago American psychology freed itself from domination by ethics, and one hundred years later it extricated itself from mental philosophy.[20] Browning has made significant contributions in identifying the implicit ethical assumptions within psychotherapy systems, as well as in seeking correctives. He is critical of the moral neutrality espoused by psychologists, but, rather than rejecting psychology, Browning proposes corrections through interdisciplinary studies in theology, ethics, and philosophy:

> The normative disciplines, however, should have the central role in specifying the final content of the normative life. If the modern sciences—especially the psychologists and psychotherapists—took this seriously, they would be far more tentative about their concepts of human nature and would turn far more frequently to the normative disciplines for consultation about their guiding images.[21]

The Polarization

There have been two distinct trends within the last decade, relative to the mixing of psychology, morality, and the church. These trends represent polarities, both of which have been institutionalized, and neither of which seems capable of bridging the interdisciplinary hurdles of theoretical and practical theology. The first stems from an overemphasis on the practical side, while the second stems from an overemphasis on the theoretical side.

In the first trend, Evangelical seminaries have moved beyond the pastoral counseling movement to the development of doctoral programs in counseling or clinical psychology and in marital and family therapy, enabling their graduates to become state-licensed. But they have yet to undertake serious interdisciplinary studies in theology, ethics, and psychology. While seminary-trained therapists are usually required to obtain master's degrees in biblical and theological studies, these programs are not significantly interdisciplinary. Such was the experience of an intern at the Needham Institute, who graduated from a seminary counseling program that had not required the reading of one theological or religious book in two years of psychological training.

The second trend, the "moral majority," has developed as a significant force in the eighties, with the endorsement of President Reagan.[22] It is a conservative church movement that addresses the perceived moral crisis in American society by insisting on definite conditions under which a person can be accepted. Because of their fervent attitudes against secularization and their fear and rejection of psychology, many of these conservative churches cut their constituents off from professional help. It is the strategy of pastoral care and counseling in these churches that is most vulnerable in this age of increased charges of clergy malpractice.

The First Clergy Malpractice Case

Apparently, the first suit against a pastor's counseling occurred more than a decade before the celebrated 1980 *Nally v. Grace Community Church of the Valley* suit discussed in the next section. According to Church Mutual Insurance Company's corporate attorney John Cleary,[23] the first one was the 1966 suit of *Carrieri v. Bush* for alienation of affection.

Unlike suits alleging that a minister has created alienation of affection through an adulterous relationship, the Carrieri suit alleged that a pastor had created a permanent alienation of affection through his counsel. When the trial court dismissed the suit, Carrieri appealed to the Washington State Supreme Court. This court reversed the dismissal, emphasizing several critical points.

First, the decision extended the interpretation of alienation beyond the traditional concepts of adultery or improper relations and spite or malice: "Conduct, without justification or excuse, coupled with a purpose or design to adversely affect the mental attitude of one spouse to the detriment of the other is the keystone of a wrongful interference with a marital relationship."[24]

Second, the decision acknowledged the protection of religious belief by the state constitution, but excluded the alleged alienation from that protection.

> One does not, under the guise of exercising religious beliefs, acquire a license to wrongfully interfere with familial relationships. Good faith and reasonable conduct are the necessary

touchstones to any qualified privilege that may arise from any invited and religiously directed family counseling, assistance, or advice. Ill will, intimidation, threats, or reckless recommendations of family separation directed toward alienating the spouses, where found to exist, nullify the privilege and project liability.[25]

Third, the court charged that Pastor Bush was guilty of interference, citing the following conversation, between pastor and husband, as an example of how the alienation was fostered.

Respondents transported Mrs. Carrieri to and from her activities with them. One evening, at about 11:30 P.M., when Pastor Bush brought Mrs. Carrieri and the children home from the day's activities, appellant confronted the pastor. In appellant's words, the following exchange took place:
"I said, 'Arnold, you know you're causing a lot of dissension in my home by keeping my wife away all the time. I asked you not to come pick her up. I believe we should go to church together. And we got along fine before she was going with your group. And there is so much dissension I asked you not to pick my wife up, to help our family instead of hindering it. . . .' Immediately his eyes got big and large and he said immediately, he said, 'No. You're full of the devil.' My wife and children were there. He said, 'She does not have to listen to you. You're full of the devil.' He said, 'I've got the gift of discernment.' And he said, 'I know all your sins. I've got the gift of discernment.' And he repeated that I was full of the devil in front of my wife and children, and my wife was crying and my children were crying. . . . He said he would continue. He said, 'Inga, we will continue to pick you up.' He said, 'Don't listen to him. I've told you many times before, don't listen to your husband.' "[26]

Nally v. Grace Community Church

The Nallys first filed suit against Grace Community Church, in Sunland, California, in March of 1980. This was the first clergy malpractice suit focusing on the quality of care provided in religious counseling. Filing on behalf of their twenty-four-year-old son, who had committed suicide one year previously, Walter and Maria Nally charged three counts. First, they charged that Pastor MacArthur and Grace Community Church had prevented Kenneth Nally from seeking professional help. Second, they charged that Grace's lay counselors were inadequately trained and unavailable. Third, the Nallys charged that MacArthur and the church ridiculed Kenneth's previous Catholic religion, thereby exacerbating his preexisting feelings of guilt, anxiety, and depression.

In the most recent of the five years of court action, a Glendale, California, Superior Court Judge dismissed the suit following five weeks of plaintiff's presentations. Before this dismissal, the suit had been dismissed in 1981 by another Superior Court Justice. In 1984 a California Appellate Court, in a 2–1 decision, reversed the lower court's ruling and prepared the way for the church and its leadership to stand trial. Grace Church appealed to the California Supreme Court to reverse the Appellate Court ruling, but they refused to hear the case. The case went back to the California Supreme Court in 1985 because the Nallys appealed for the case to be reopened.

The case has further pushed clergy and churches into the spotlight of public discontent and litigious solutions. It has prepared the courts, the public, lawyers, and plaintiffs for the reality of further litigation against the church and its clergy. This can be seen through listening to the comments and opinions of judges, theologians, Christian psychologists, pastoral counselors, and attorneys.

The dissenting California Appellate Judge, who was overruled in a 2–1 decision that mandated the Grace Church trial, stated that he could not rule out the future possibility of a legitimate case.

> I am not saying that a church under any conceivable set of facts could never be liable for the intentional infliction of emotional distress. I am saying that in the case at bench, through the proper and fair application of the statutorily created summary judgment procedures, there are no triable issues of fact upon which to base liability under any theory alleged, including intentional infliction of emotional distress.[27]

Many within the ranks of church leadership have expressed the conviction that church and clergy should not be exempted from professional malpractice. This segment supports legal standards with a minimal quality of care and mandatory referral procedures. Dr. James Ewing, Executive of the American Association of Pastoral Counselors (AAPC), was disappointed that the California Superior Court decided (May 1985) to dismiss the Grace Church suit on the basis of the church-state issue rather than on the merits of the case. He said:

> I feel that the court sidestepped the key issue, which is what the public should expect from pastoral counselors and what stan-

dards should be given. . . . There is ambivalent ground between the church and state, and someday someone needs to plow that ground.[28]

Newton Malony, pastoral counselor, psychologist, and past president of the American Psychological Association's Division of Psychologists Interested in Religious Issues, expressed a similar opinion. Following the 1985 dismissal of the Nally case, he said:

> I have never quite bought the position that there is an absolute church-state issue. It seems to me there are some minimal concerns for the integrity of human life that should apply to all counselors . . . the state has a right to expect certain standards of care.[29]

Theologians such as Fuller Seminary professor Samuel Southard, reflecting on the Grace Community suit, contend that many ministers engage incompetently in counseling that extends them far beyond the New Testament conception of pastoral duties. The minister should not invoke his or her pastoral calling and privilege to cover psychological counseling which goes beyond pastoral duties. From this perspective, the problem is seen as one in which pastoral authority has been extended too far, rather than one in which legitimate authority has been usurped. Theologians like Southard favor a new perspective on pastoral care and counseling. According to this model, ministers should continue to benefit from psychological knowledge to increase their competence, but without the predominance of a psychological agenda, since their primary competence is in theology. The minister should become a moral and spiritual guide who is knowledgeable about psychological factors, and a team member working with psychotherapists rather than trying to replace them.

Attorneys, too, have responded to the Grace litigation. Aware of consumer protection and the central role of public opinion in court decisions, and skeptical about the logic of an unlimited exemption under church-state defense argumentation, many lawyers will continue to target the manner in which some churches and clergy conduct their ministry. Many will come to the same conclusion as Ben Zion Bergman: "First amendment protection is not absolute and inviolate but is subject to being outweighed by the state's duty to protect its citizens." (See next-to-last paragraph of chapter 2.)

John Cleary, corporate counsel for Church Mutual Insurance

Company and an analyst of legal trends in the church, predicts a gradual change both in people's willingness to sue their clergy and in the willingness of the courts to try such cases, similar to a gradual increased willingness to try the church on other matters. He says:

> In the future, I expect to see more suits of this nature filed. I don't expect to see large verdicts rendered. Gradually, there may be some inroads to the traditional doctrines of law which allow an action to exist, and ultimately a verdict may be paid in a clergy malpractice lawsuit. I say this not because I look with disfavor on the facts of the cases that I have handled; rather, I say it because, in the past, that is the way it has always happened. Remember, at one time you could not sue or recover a judgment from a church. It now happens on a regular basis, although it happened over a period of fifty years.[30]

The Church as Defendant: Pending Litigation

Cleary also points out that it will probably take several years before the courts reduce their resistance to accepting cases alleging clergy malpractice. Therefore, attorneys will continue to design their charges in a legally acceptable manner.[31] Accordingly, at present, clergy suits are being filed in three general categories: (1) sexual misconduct and abuse, (2) breach of oral contract (counseling), and (3) invasion of privacy, through publication of private facts, libel, or slander.

Sexual Misconduct and Abuse

Churches and clergy, like psychologists, are experiencing significant increases in suits alleging sexual misconduct. The charges include adulterous conduct, verbalized sexual desires, sexual assault on minor children, and sexual abuse resulting from improper supervision of church activities, day-care centers, or church-related schools. The costly nature of many of these suits will be discussed in chapter 7.

Breach of Oral Contract (Counseling)

In an unusual sexual misconduct case, a Los Angeles man is suing his temple and rabbi for breach-of-counseling contract. A couple, both members of a Los Angeles Jewish temple, received intermittent marital counseling from one of their rabbis over a period of four and a half years. In his suit, the now-divorced husband alleges that the temple and the rabbi "failed to provide constructive marriage counseling."[32] The suit alleges that the temple failed to inform the husband that the rabbi was engaging in sexual intercourse with his wife during this time. In fact, the temple allegedly withheld secured explicit videotaped evidence of his wife's and other temple wives' sexual affairs with the rabbi.

The plaintiff's attorney is seeking to hold the rabbi and the temple accountable for the violation of standards adhered to by marital therapists in Los Angeles. They contend that the rabbi and the temple were providing a secular counseling activity, under proper authorization of the California Business and Professions Code, Section 17300.1, and that the rabbi and the temple offered marital counseling which led the plaintiff to conclude that he was receiving a secular service equivalent to similar services offered in the Greater Los Angeles community. The original complaint includes a statement about the standard of care which the plaintiff believed the temple and the rabbi were offering: "Counseling rendered would be within the standard of practice of marital counselors in the community of the City of Los Angeles."[33]

Invasion of Privacy

There are several types of invasion-of-privacy litigations stemming from various church ministries: sacred confession, church discipline, and counseling and discipline.

In March of 1984, a Tulsa, Oklahoma, jury decided for the plaintiff in a celebrated church discipline case. The Church of Christ of Collinsville, Oklahoma, had publicly expelled a woman for alleged sexual involvement with the town's divorced mayor. She contended that her request to withdraw from the church before publication of her private life was denied. Her attorney successfully pleaded two counts of invasion of privacy, both publication of private facts and intrusion upon seclusion, as well as intentional infliction of emotional distress. The court award included $205,000 for actual damages, $185,000 for punitive damages, $44,737 prejudgment interest from date of filing, 15 percent interest till paid in full, and all attorneys' fees and court costs.[34]

A similar suit was filed against Fairview Church of Christ, Garden Grove, California, by an expelled woman who had been a member for nineteen years. In a letter prepared by the pastor and board and read to the congregation during a January 1984 morning service, Jan Brown was disfellowshipped. In her complaint, Brown charged libel, slander, invasion of privacy, and the intentional infliction of emotional distress.[35] As in the Collinsville church case, the plaintiff was not allowed to withdraw privately.

In another invasion-of-privacy suit, a San Jose, California, man alleges that his therapist, a Ph.D. California-licensed marital and family therapist who was also a board member at his church, revealed intimate details of his sexual life to the pastor and other board members. The plaintiff contends that the confidential information was obtained during a time when he was paying the therapist for his services. The suit further charges that this information was publicly released in April 1983 as the basis for excommunicating him. Professional malpractice, conspiracy, extortion, and blackmail are also included in the delineation of charges.[36]

The San Jose defendants petitioned the court for a dismissal, contending that the suit "is without merit and that there are no triable issues of material fact insofar as the controversy which exists between John R. Kelly and said defendants is ecclesiastical in nature and not subject to the jurisdiction of this court."[37] On September 11, 1985, California Supreme Court Judge Peter Stone denied this request for summary judgment dismissal,[38] further advancing the suit to the trial stage.

Recently, a convicted embezzler filed an invasion-of-privacy suit against a Tiburon (California) Episcopal church. She contends that the priest divulged her confidential and sacred confession of a crime to the local police. While the criminal court judge protected the minister's disclosure of the confidential information, the woman confessant now contends that St. Stephen's Episcopal Church misrepresented the "secrecy, sanctity, and sacramental nature of confessions made to them."[39]

Summary

Churches and clergy have been sued and will continue to be sued for liabilities arising out of the manner in which they conduct their professional duties. Public pressures, arising from consumer discontent, will in all likelihood gradually erode court resistance to directly trying cases charging clergy malpractice. Until that time, however, attorneys and plaintiffs will continue to design their cases in ways acceptable to the court.

2

What the Law Says

The extent to which clergy are legally responsible to the state for their actions is debatable. Two examples of this debate follow.

On the one hand, some legal experts assert that the separation of church and state is absolute and that ministers cannot be subject to legal scrutiny or censure. While there may be many in society who would like to tell clergy what they may or may not say or do, the Constitution provides for the protection of religion from the state, and that right must be safeguarded. The first essay, by Samuel E. Ericsson, represents this point of view.

Ericsson contends that there can be no such thing as clergy malpractice because malpractice is a term that applies to deviation from legal or professional standards. Since clergy are not, and cannot be, regulated by society, "clergy malpractice" is a misnomer. It is a "new theory," as the title of Ericsson's article suggests. He would add it is not only a new theory but non-theory, in the sense that it has no precedent and violates the separation of church and state.

Ericsson was the defense counsel in the celebrated Nally v. Grace Community Church case that was dismissed by a California judge on May 16, 1985. Ericsson based his defense solely on the position noted. The judge concurred and concluded that for the court to venture into the area of judging religion would be dangerous.

On the other hand, some legal experts contend that while the state has no right to regulate the "religious" activities of ministers, it does have the right, and the obligation, to protect its *citizens from harm, and in that role it should regulate the "non-religious" activities that clergy perform.*

The second essay, by Ben Zion Bergman, defends this position. Bergman contends that no one would excuse people for not having driving licenses or for reckless driving simply because they were ministers or rabbis. He suggests there should be minimal standards of care to which clergy should be held responsible. He compares clergy to psychologists in the same way that general physicians are related to specialists: one should know when to refer to the other.

Thus, for Bergman, malpractice is a viable term and should be used in regulating ministerial behavior. He acknowledges the importance of separating church and state but asserts the right of the state to regulate nonreligious clerical activity and to establish a minimum standard of care to which all citizens are entitled.

I. "Clergy Malpractice": Ramifications of a New Theory

Samuel E. Ericsson

Perhaps more than any other branch of the law, the law of torts is a battleground of social theory.[1] This essay will examine the implications of a recently introduced legal theory known as "clergy malpractice." This new theory is so inextricably entwined with ecclesiastical, spiritual, and doctrinal matters that the judicial system cannot competently deal with it, nor can it constitutionally do so.

The first part briefly examines the theory of clergy malpractice in light of key elements of a cause of action for negligence. The second part reviews some ancillary consequences of the theory, including its impact on the doctrine of the priest-penitent privilege and the imposition of a duty to refer. The third part examines certain statutory exemptions. The last part addresses some constitutional issues raised by the theory.

It is not suggested that the law provide special or favored treatment for the religious community in the area of torts or that the now generally discarded concept of charitable immunity be resurrected. The religious community should not expect special treatment in cases where the conduct in question has little or nothing to do with its religious or spiritual mission. Thus, liability arising out of traditional theories of personal injury, false imprisonment, battery, assault, or duties arising out of property ownership should not differ simply because the defendant happens to be a religious organization or a clergyperson.

One question addressed is whether "clergy malpractice" is simply another legal theory against a profession, akin to theories of legal malpractice in the field of law and medical malpractice in the field of medicine. It will be shown, however, that it is the uniqueness of the "service rendered" by the religious community to those who seek counsel from it that sets this new theory apart from other seemingly related torts.

It should also be noted that although moral and legal obligations often coincide, they are separate and distinct and must be treated as such. Moral obligations do not always rise to the level of a legal duty. Thus, clergy have many duties *qua* clergy to their parishioners. However, to the extent that these duties flow from a religious and spiritual mission, it is not the proper function of the state to act as the enforcer of those duties through the courts.

In the fall of 1979, a story made the rounds in the insurance and religious media that a clergyman had been sued and held liable in a "clergy malpractice" case. The story was initiated by the insurance industry, apparently to generate interest in a new product known as "clergy malpractice insurance."[2]

In March 1980, a much-publicized suit was brought in Burbank, California, by the parents of Ken Nally, a twenty-four-year-old seminary student who committed suicide in 1979.[3] The Nallys sued Grace Community Church, the largest Protestant congregation in Los Angeles County, its pastor, and staff, alleging in three counts clergy malpractice, negligence, and outrageous conduct. In a media blitz accompanying the filing of the lawsuit, plaintiffs' counsel indicated that this was the first case of its kind in California.[4]

In the first count, the parents alleged that the pastor and staff had counseled their son to read the Bible, pray, listen to taped sermons, and counsel with church counselors. They alleged that the defendants were aware that their son was depressed and had suicidal tendencies and was in need of professional psychiatric and psychological care. Notwithstanding such knowledge, plaintiffs alleged that the church and its staff discouraged and effectively prevented their son from seeking professional help outside the church.

In the second count, the complaint alleged that the defendants were negligent in the training, selection, and hiring of its "lay spiritual counselors." The count additionally alleged that these counselors were unavailable when Nally requested counseling.

The third count alleged that the defendants ridiculed, disparaged, and denigrated the Catholic religion and the faith and belief of the decedent's parents, and that this exacerbated Nally's preexisting feelings of guilt, anxiety, and depression. It was further alleged that defendants effectively required the decedent to spend time in isolation, thereby preventing him from contacting or consulting with persons not affiliated with the church, and that this proximately caused the young man to take his own life.

Defendants' lengthy demurrer to the complaint was denied on the grounds that certain conduct implied in the complaint—namely, the charge that Nally had been effectively prevented from obtaining professional help—fell within the parameters of tort law.

Deposition testimony showed that the young man was seen by at least eight physicians, psychologists, and psychiatrists in the few months prior to his death. In fact, Grace Church, its staff, and members repeatedly encouraged Nally to keep his appointments with the professionals and even made some of the appointments for him. A number of these professionals, along with other members of the church and staff, recommended psychiatric hospitalization to the young man, but to no avail. The testimony also indicated that the same recommendations were made to the parents.

Some Threshold Problems of Definition

The traditional elements necessary to state a cause of action in negligence have been summarily stated by Professor Prosser.[5] Although negligence is simply one kind of conduct, a cause of action founded upon negligence from which liability will follow requires more than conduct. There must be a legally recognizable duty and a breach of that duty causally connected to the subsequent injury resulting in actual damage. This essay will not review the new malpractice theory in light of each of these elements, but rather will deal primarily with the concept of duty and some of the problems of proof related thereto.

In examining the concept of duty, there exists a threshold

issue of defining the nature of the conduct underlying the theory. The better label for the conduct may in fact be "spiritual counseling malpractice" where the dispute focuses on counseling rendered by a member of the clergy in meeting the spiritual, emotional, and religious needs of the counselee.

The difficulty facing the courts in constructing a duty in these cases is amplified by the confusion and lack of definition as to what falls within the parameters of spiritual as opposed to psychological or psychiatric counseling. What is the nature of the problem plaguing the counselee? Is it "poor mental health" or "poor moral health"? And how shall a court determine, as a matter of law, whether a counselee's problem is "sin"-related or its psychological equivalent? How can one draw the line and where should it be drawn?

It is impossible to separate the "cure of minds" from the "cure of souls." An unstated and patently invalid assumption of spiritual counseling malpractice is that clean lines exist delineating the realm of religion from the realm of psychology and psychiatry. For nearly 2,000 years pastors, priests, rabbis, and other spiritual counselors in churches have been providing the balm for those suffering from depression, guilt, and anxiety.

Attempts to delineate the functions of the clergy as counselors from those of psychiatrists or psychologists—as if one is religion and the other is medicine—have been rebutted by leading psychiatrists and psychologists, including Sigmund Freud and Carl Jung.

> Now they [the courts!] view reading the Talmud or the Bible as a matter of religion, but reading Freud or Spock as a matter of mental health. Thus we have transformed the cure of souls into the cure of minds, and our prohibitions against clerical coercion into our prescriptions for clinical coercion.
>
> In short, I contend that we now classify many medical acts as scientific when, in fact, they are moral, and that *we classify many psychiatric acts as medical when, in fact, they are religious.* These opinions, which may seem strange or even outlandish today, are actually the opinions of the "founding fathers" of modern psychiatry.
>
> Toward the end of his life, Sigmund Freud asserted, "I have assumed . . . that psychoanalysis is not a specialized branch of medicine. I cannot see how it is possible to dispute this." His reason for so classifying psychoanalysis was "[t]he case of analysis differs from that of [a specialized branch of medicine]. . . . [T]he only subject-matter of psychoanalysis is the mental processes of

human beings and it is only in human beings that it can be studied."

If psychoanalysis is not a branch of medicine, what is it a branch of? According to Freud, *it is a branch of religion:* "[T]he words *secular pastoral worker* might well serve as a general formula for describing the function [of] the analyst. . . . We do not seek to bring [the patient] relief by receiving him into the catholic, protestant or socialist community. We seek rather to enrich him from his own internal sources. . . Such activity as this is *pastoral work* in the best sense of the words."

Carl Jung, the co-architect of modern psychiatry, was even more emphatic in rejecting the medical pretensions of psychotherapy (and psychiatry), and in *reiterating the essentially religious character of soul-curing:* "[In] most cases the sufferer consults the doctor in the first place because he supposes himself to be physically ill. . . . That is why patients force the psychotherapist into *the role of a priest,* and expect and demand of him that he shall free them from their distress. *That is why we psychotherapists must occupy ourselves with problems which, strictly speaking, belong to the theologian."*

. . . We now face a serious problem concerning classification not in just one crucial area, but in two. Our forebearers went astray in categorizing some people—blacks—as non-persons; but *at least they recognized religion when they saw it, and demarcated ecclesiastical from secular institutions* and interventions correctly and wisely.

We go astray in categorizing some people—mental patients—as non-persons; and *we no longer recognize* religion when we see it, demarcating medical from moral institutions and interventions incorrectly and stupidly.[6]

Renowned psychiatrist Karl Menninger, founder of the Menninger Clinic, believes that mental health and moral health are identical and that the recognition of the reality of "sin" offers to the suffering, struggling anxious world a real hope.[7] O. Hobart Mowrer, a noted research psychologist who has served as president of the American Psychologist Association, challenged the entire field of psychiatry, declaring it a failure, and sought to refute its fundamental Freudian presuppositions.[8]

In spite of the antireligious prejudice of modern psychology, even a prominent psychologist like Mowrer appreciates the psychological necessity of accepting sin:

For several decades we psychologists looked upon the whole matter of sin and moral accountability as a great incubus and acclaimed our liberation from it as epoch-making. But at length we have discovered that to be "free" in this sense, i.e., to have the excuse of being "sick" rather than sinful, is to court the danger of also becoming lost. This danger is, I believe, betokened by the widespread interest in Existentialism which we are presently witnessing. In becoming amoral, ethically neutral, and "free," we have cut the very roots of our being; lost our deepest sense of self-hood and identity; and with neurotics themselves, find ourselves asking: "Who am I?"[9]

The great benefit of the doctrine of sin is that it reintroduces responsibility for one's own behavior, responsibility for changing as well as giving meaning to the human condition. Mowrer describes the benefits from the acceptance of sin:

> [R]ecovery (constructive change, redemption) is most assuredly attained, not by helping a person reject and rise above his sins, but by helping him *accept them*. This is the paradox which we have not at all understood and which is the very crux of the problem. Just so long as a person lives under the shadow of real, unacknowledged, and unexpiated guilt, he *cannot* (if he has any character at all) "accept himself"; and all *our* efforts to reassure and accept him will avail nothing. He will continue to hate himself and to suffer the inevitable consequences of self-hatred. But the moment he (with or without "assistance") begins to accept his guilt and sinfulness, the possibility of radical reformation opens up; and with this, the individual may legitimately, though not without pain and effort, pass from deep, pervasive self-rejection and self-torture to a new freedom, of self-respect and peace.[10]

The difficulty of attempting to categorize psychiatry and psychology as separate from the religious and spiritual realms is further reflected in *Psychology as Religion: The Cult of Self-Worship.*[11] The thesis of the book is that "psychology as religion" exists in great strength throughout the United States and that this "religion" is hostile to most religions.[12] In fact, in many instances "psychology as religion is deeply anti-Christian."[13]

In counseling malpractice cases, the issue facing the courts may thus become one of choosing between competing religious dogmas. While the courts do deal with issues beyond their own expertise and discipline, those issues are empirical in nature. The issues raised in clergy counseling cases are not empirical, but religious. They are not conducive to judicial review because they lack objective standards.

A second problem facing the courts under the spiritual counseling theory will be to identify the scope and nature of church-related counseling. As a matter of law, what constitutes spiritual guidance and counseling? Does it include the one-time, five-minute emergency telephone call that pastors and counselors may receive in the course of their day from distressed individuals, members as well as non-members of their congregations? Does it include confessions? Or is "spiritual counseling" limited to formal office visits where a pastor or other counselor counsels, notebook in hand, at a scheduled time, on a regular basis, over a long period of time? In the *Nally* case, the complaint alleged that the church staff failed to make themselves available to the counselee when he requested their counsel and guidance. The courts will thus be called upon to determine the scope of a church's duty to be available to counselees.

The issue of availability of church-related counseling in turn raises other issues, including some doctrinal judgment calls. For example, in his parable of the good Samaritan, Christ made it imperative that Christians show mercy to all those in need who may come across their path (Luke 10:25–37). Thus, many churches and counselors may not feel that they have the option of other professionals to select and screen their counselees, determining the availability of their services on such factors as ability to pay, office hours, or scheduling.

However, scripture teaches that Christians should not waste time on those who are unruly, undisciplined, and repeatedly reject counsel (see, e.g., 2 Thess. 3:14–15). Can the courts avoid second-guessing decisions by churches as to whether they should have been more or less available to counselees in any given case? Will the duty to be available be the same for all churches and counseling ministries? Or will the duty depend upon such variables as the size of the congregation and the staff trained for counseling?

A third area in which the courts must become involved is determining whether the duty owed to a counselee would be any different depending upon the counselor's ecclesiastical office and the authority or function flowing from such office. All religions identify various positions, offices, or titles reflecting a person's authority and service. For example, the Roman Catholic Church has nuns, mother superiors, brothers, fathers, priests, bishops, cardinals, and the pope. Protestants identify ministers such as evangelists, pastors, elders, deacons, youth ministers, and Sunday school teachers. Other religions have their apostles, prophets, rabbis, vicars, divine masters, seers, and even presidents.

The relationship a counselee has with a counselor may de-

pend upon the nature and function of the office of the counselor. Arguably, the various offices of a given faith are not to be
treated legally alike in counseling cases, any more than all those
in the medical profession are treated alike in medical malpractice cases, where it makes a difference whether the person is
a nurse, surgeon, orderly, anesthesiologist, or laboratory techni-
cian.[14]

Fourth, as in other "professional" malpractice, the courts
must review the training and competence of individual counselors.[15] This will present the court with a host of new problems.
Shall the review be limited to the training received in secular
institutions on secular subjects, such as psychology, psychiatry,
and mental health counseling? Would a degree in clinical psychology from an accredited university provide the desired training?

> To date, psychiatry has not clearly defined the skills, knowledge,
> and attitudes that the psychiatrist-in-training must demonstrate in
> order to be certified as competent. It is our belief that the profes-
> sion can no longer avoid beginning the difficult, often emotion-
> laden task of specifying what a psychiatrist should know and be
> able to do.[16]

If the professional jury is still out on what secular professionals should know and be able to do in the area of counseling,
what standards should the court look to when faced with the
issue of the competence and training of church counselors?
Shall a counselor's library be reviewed to see which books are
used in counseling individuals? If the Bible is the primary source
used in spiritual counseling, shall the court determine the depth
of training in scriptures that the counselor has had, and whether
the training was adequate to deal with the specific nature of the
counselee's problem?

Aside from secular training, a Christian counselor's competence may depend upon many "spiritual" qualifications such as
the counselor's spiritual gifts and his or her spiritual maturity.
The Bible indicates that spiritual counseling is the work of the
Holy Spirit and that effective counseling cannot be done apart
from him.[17] The Spirit endows each believer with a spiritual gift
or gifts, some of which may have a direct bearing on the counselor's ability and effectiveness (see, e.g., Eph. 4:7–13; Rom.
12:3–8; 1 Cor. 12:1–11). Might someone with a number of key
spiritual gifts, such as wisdom, knowledge, or exhortation, be
held to a higher standard of care (akin to a specialist) than other

spiritual counselors who may have been endowed with fewer, if any, of these specific gifts? There is no doubt that all religions consider spiritual maturity a significant factor in evaluating a counselor's competence. A secular court, however, may decide to apply purely secular criteria, such as that of clinical psychology, and dismiss the religious standard as irrelevant and inapplicable.

A fifth area facing the court relates to the content of the counsel given by the pastor or church counselor. For example, the *Nally* complaint alleged that the counselors at the church told Nally to read the Bible, pray, and listen to taped sermons and church counselors while, on the other hand, they allegedly dissuaded and discouraged him from seeking professional psychiatric or psychological help. As a practical matter, wholly apart from the constitutional prohibitions, the courts are not equipped to evaluate the content of the counsel provided by a church to those individuals who voluntarily embrace the doctrinal stance of the church.[18]

It is inevitable that in making the courts the battleground for evaluating the content of the counseling, two inherently inconsistent worldviews will clash. The secular humanist proponents will echo the views set forth, for example, in the Humanist Manifesto that

> traditional theism, especially in the prayer-hearing God, assumed to love and care for persons, to hear and understand their prayers, and to be able to do something about them, is an unproved and outmoded faith. Salvationism, based on mere affirmation, still appears as harmful, diverting people with false hopes of heaven hereafter. Reasonable minds look to other means for survival.[19]

The opposite worldview, of course, is that of the religious community as seen in the Christian belief in a personal God, who cares and answers prayer and has spoken through his Word—the Holy Scripture.

Thus, the theory of spiritual counseling malpractice or clergy malpractice raises mind-boggling implications considering what the judicial system is being asked to do. Further, it is clear that clergy malpractice is not akin to other professional malpractice concepts.

Ancillary Consequences

Historically, the law has recognized certain types of communications as being privileged from disclosure, including communications between pastor and penitent.[20] This privilege recognizes the great need in society that individuals may confess matters to the clergy free from fear that the matter will ever be disclosed to others. The California Supreme Court has held that the clergy-penitent privilege is absolute. In *In re Lifschutz*,[21] the court dealt with the issue of the constitutionality of the clergy-penitent privilege. The defendant, a psychiatrist, contended that the privilege was unconstitutional because it distinguished between clergy and psychiatrists/psychotherapists. The court noted that the clergy-penitent privilege fostered a "sanctuary for the disclosure of emotional distresses," adding:

> Realistically, the statutory privilege must be recognized as basically an explicit accommodation by the secular state to strongly held religious tenets of a large segment of its citizenry. As the Law Revision Commission Comment accompanying the adoption of California's current privilege explains: "At least one underlying reason seems to be that *the law will not compel a clergyman to violate—nor punish him for refusing to violate—the tenets of his church which require him to maintain secrecy as to confidential statements made to him in the course of his religious duties.*" Wigmore, in his treatise, similarly relates the purpose of the privilege in a question-and-answer format: "Does the penitential relation deserve recognition and countenance? In a state where toleration of religion exists by law, and where a substantial part of the community professes a religion practicing a confessional system, this question must be answered in the affirmative."[22]

Clergy should not be placed in a position where they would be punished for refusing to violate the confidentiality of the penitent's communication. If the courts adopt the theory of spiritual counseling malpractice, clergy will feel pressured to disclose to the family or others the contents of discussions with a counselee with the understanding that confidentiality will be honored. Often counselees desire to protect their own reputations, as well as those of their families and others, in discussing a problem with their pastor. If the courts impose on the clergy a duty to disclose, counselees might not be as candid. As a practical matter, effective counseling by the clergy would be seriously hampered.

Some might assert that churches can always buy counseling malpractice insurance if they want to fulfill their mission to be good Samaritans to those with spiritual and emotional problems. However, the argument for spiritual counseling malpractice insurance overlooks the implications this has for the clergy-penitent privilege. It is well settled that an insured has a duty to cooperate with the insurer in defending a lawsuit.[23] Without such cooperation and assistance, the insurer is severely handicapped and may in some instances be absolutely precluded from advancing any defense. In a case where the penitent/counselee is not available to testify, the defense may hinge on a pastor's disclosing confidential communications. The pastor who refuses to make such a disclosure might be held to have violated the duty to cooperate with the insurer and thereby release the insurer from the obligation to defend the suit. Thus, malpractice insurance may not be an effective protection.

In addition to the problems raised by the implied duty to disclose contents of confidential communications, the theory of spiritual counseling malpractice also raises by inference a duty on the part of the clergy to refer the most difficult problem counselees to professional specialists, such as psychiatrists, psychologists, and other mental health workers. In the medical field, for instance, there is a duty on the part of a physician or surgeon who is a general practitioner to refer a patient to a specialist or recommend the assistance of a specialist if, under the circumstances, a reasonably careful and skillful general practitioner would do so.[24] However, the nature of pastoral counseling may bar the creation of any such duty. In the Christian religion, for example, the role of a pastor is often described as that of a shepherd, caring for a troubled, discouraged, and fearful flock (see Ps. 23; John 10:1–29; 21:15–17). Pastors are under a mandate to protect those in their care from counsel that might undermine their faith (see, e.g., Ps. 1; 2 Tim. 4:1–4; Titus 1). In any given case, there may not be a professional psychiatrist, psychologist, or other mental health worker who is supportive of the doctrinal stance of the church. It would seem untenable that a legal duty would be created forcing such churches and their clergy to refer their troubled members to professionals who may, in fact, be hostile to the members' faith.[25]

The propriety of imposing on the clergy a duty to refer leads to the question of whether the courts should create a reciprocal legal duty on the part of mental health professionals, such as psychiatrists and psychologists, to refer to clergy *all* spiritual cases—the simple as well as the serious—with a consequent liability for failing to refer their patients to the "proper" clergy in the event of a suicide? Should the moral model take a backseat to the medical model in counseling?

Legislative Exemptions and Some Constitutional Implications

The practical ramifications of developing criteria by which the courts will judge the qualifications, competence, and content of counseling by clergy are far-reaching. States such as California have chosen not to establish statutory criteria by which to evaluate the competence of those who counsel under the auspices of their church or synagogue. In fact, several California statutes expressly exempt such counselors from licensing requirements. For example, provisions governing the licensing of medical professionals in California state that the act shall not be construed so as to "regulate, prohibit, or apply to any kind of treatment of prayer, nor interfere in any way with the practice of religion."[26]

Similar language is found in the law governing licensing of psychiatrists and psychiatric technicians that provides that the act "does not prohibit the provisions of services regulated herein, with or without compensation or personal profit, when done by the tenets of any well-recognized church or denomination."[27] Another example of the exemption of these counselors from state-defined criteria is found in the licensing of marriage, family, child, and domestic counselors, which provides that the act "shall not apply to any priest, rabbi, or minister of the gospel of any religious denomination when performing counseling services as part of his pastoral or professional duties."[28] However, the law does not define what "counseling services" entail.

Exemption provisions, such as those in California, indicate that the legislature has recognized that the subject matter of counseling by the clergy may often be the same as that facing the licensed and regulated professional. However, the legislature, through the exemption provisions, has recognized that the secular state is not equipped to ascertain the competence of counseling when performed by those affiliated with religious organizations.

Constitutional Issues

Judicial review of counseling by the clergy will inevitably draw the courts into the dangerous ground of evaluating the truth or error of the counseling given. As indicated in the first section, the courts are not equipped as a practical matter to deal with the issues in this arena, and it is questionable whether they are constitutionally permitted to render the kind of decisions called for in these types of cases.

The most significant decision by the United States Supreme Court on this issue is *United States v. Ballard.*[29] *Ballard* involved the "I Am" movement, founded by Guy and Edna Ballard and their son, Donald. The Ballards were indicted and convicted in federal district court for using, and conspiring to use, the mails to defraud. The Ballards represented that they could, by virtue of supernatural powers, cure persons of diseases normally classified as curable, as well as heal those with diseases ordinarily classified by the medical profession as incurable. The Ballards further represented that they had in fact cured hundreds of persons afflicted with these diseases and ailments.

The trial court instructed the jury that they were not permitted to decide whether any of the religious claims made by the Ballards were actually true. The central question for the jury was whether the Ballards honestly and in good faith *believed* their claims to be true.[30]

The Ninth Circuit Court of Appeals reversed the conviction and granted a new trial on the grounds that restricting the issue to that of good faith was error.[31] The Supreme Court granted *certiorari* and reversed the Ninth Circuit, holding that the trial court ruled properly when it withheld from the jury all questions concerning the truth or falsity of the religious beliefs or doctrines of the Ballards.[32]

Writing for the majority, Justice Douglas stated that the First Amendment forbids the courts to examine the truth or verity of religious representations.

> The First Amendment has a dual aspect. It not only "forestalls compulsion by law of the acceptance of any creed or the practice of any form of worship" but also "safeguards the free exercise of the chosen form of religion." ... "Thus the Amendment embraces two concepts—freedom to believe and freedom to act. The first is absolute but, in the nature of things, the second cannot be." Freedom of thought, which includes freedom of religious belief, is basic in a society of free men. ... It embraces the right to

maintain theories of life and of death and of the hereafter which are rank heresy to followers of the orthodox faiths. Heresy trials are foreign to our Constitution. Men may believe what they cannot prove. They may not be put to the proof of their religious doctrines or beliefs. Religious experiences which are as real as life to some may be incomprehensible to others. Yet the fact that they may be beyond the ken of mortals does not mean that they can be made suspect before the law. Many take their gospel from the New Testament. But it would hardly be supposed that they could be tried before a jury charged with the duty of determining whether those teachings contained false representations. The miracles of the New Testament, the Divinity of Christ, life after death, the power of prayer are deep in the religious convictions of many. If one could be sent to jail because a jury in a hostile environment found those teachings false, little indeed would be left of religious freedom. The Fathers of the Constitution were not unaware of the varied and extreme views of religious sects, of the violence of disagreement among them, and of the lack of any one religious creed on which all men would agree. They fashioned a charter of government which envisaged the widest possible toleration of conflicting views. Man's relation to his God was made no concern of the state. He was granted the right to worship as he pleased and to answer to no man for the verity of his religious views. The religious views espoused by respondents might seem incredible, if not preposterous, to most people. But if those doctrines are subject to trial before a jury charged with finding their truth or falsity, then the same can be done with the religious beliefs of any sect. When the triers of fact undertake that task, they enter a forbidden domain. The First Amendment does not select any one group or any one type of religion for preferred treatment. It puts them all in that position.[33]

The analysis by Justice Douglas would apply with equal force to clergy malpractice cases. The fact that *Ballard* involved criminal fraud, rather than a civil action, should make no difference. In either case, the First Amendment protects the communication of beliefs that cannot be proved and that "might seem incredible, if not preposterous, to most people." Thus, under *Ballard,* the only issue for the secular courts would be a determination of whether the asserted religious belief was sincerely held.

Justice Jackson, in dissent, would have gone even further than the majority by also withholding from the jury the question of whether the Ballards honestly believed their religious claims to be true. He would have dismissed all charges and "have done with this business of judicially examining other peoples' faiths."[34] Justice Jackson found it difficult to reconcile the majority's conclusion with traditional religious freedoms on four grounds. First, as a matter of either practice or philosophy, he could not see how the Court could separate an issue as to what is believed from considerations as to what is believable. He asked, "How can the government prove these persons know something to be false which it cannot prove to be false?"[35]

Second, he observed that any inquiry into intellectual honesty in religion raises profound psychological problems. In quoting William James, he noted that it is religious experience, not theology or ceremony, that keeps religion going:

> If you ask what these experiences are, they are conversations with the unseen, voices and visions, responses to prayer, changes of heart, deliverances from fear, inflowings of help, assurances of support, whenever certain persons set their own internal attitude in certain appropriate ways.[36]

Justice Jackson also noted that religious liberty includes the right to communicate such experiences to others and presents juries with an impossible task of separating dreams from real happenings.

> Such experiences, like some tones and colors, have existence for one, but none at all for another. They cannot be verified to the minds of those whose field of consciousness does not include religious insight. When one comes to trial which turns on any aspect of religious belief or representation, unbelievers among his judges are likely not to understand and are almost certain not to believe him.[37]

Third, all religious representation is based on some element of faith.

> All schools of religious thought make enormous assumptions, generally on the basis of revelations authenticated by some sign or miracle. The appeal in such matters is to a very different plane of credulity than is invoked by representations of secular fact in commerce. Some who profess belief in the Bible read literally what others read as allegory or metaphor, as they read Aesop's Fables.[38]

A fourth observation was that the chief wrong committed by false prophets is not to be measured in financial terms but is on the mental and spiritual plane.

> There are those who hunger and thirst after higher values which they feel wanting in their humdrum lives. They live in mental confusion or moral anarchy and seek vaguely for truth and

beauty and moral support. When they are deluded and then disillusioned, cynicism and confusion follow. The wrong of these things, as I see it, is not in the money the victims part with half as much as in the mental and spiritual poison they get. But that is precisely the thing the Constitution put beyond the reach of the prosecutor, for the price of freedom of religion or of speech or of the press is that we must put up with, and even pay for, a good deal of rubbish.

Prosecutions of this character easily could degenerate into religious persecution. I do not doubt that religious leaders may be convicted of fraud for making false representations on matters other than faith or experience, as for example if one represents that funds are being used to construct a church when in fact they are being used for personal purposes. But that is not this case, which reaches into wholly dangerous ground.[39]

Although the majority was not willing to go along with Justice Jackson's proposal to do away with the "business of judicially examining other peoples' faith," the Supreme Court may be more inclined to do so today in view of the broadening of the traditional definition of religion.[40] The early definition of "religion" centered on theism, but in the latter half of the twentieth century there has been a shift away from that position, as the court has broadened the definition of what is "religion" for free exercise purposes.[41]

The Court's redefinition of "religious belief" came primarily in a series of cases involving conscientious objectors. In 1933, the Court upheld the conviction of an alien under an act that required aliens applying for naturalization to take an oath affirming a willingness to bear arms, regardless of their opinions or beliefs.[42] Justice Hughes stated in his dissent that:

The essence of religion is belief in a relation to God involving duties superior to those arising from any human relation. . . . One cannot speak of religious liberty, with proper appreciation of its essential and historical significance, without assuming the existence of a belief in supreme allegiance to the will of God.[43]

This traditional definition was set aside in *United States v. Seeger,*[44] where the Court reversed two of three convictions under the Universal Military Training and Service Act. The Court held that the test of "religious" belief within the meaning of the Act was whether it was a "sincere and meaningful belief which occupies in the life of its possessor a place parallel to that filled by the God of those who admittedly qualify for the exemption."[45] In *Seeger,* the Court noted that while it could not examine the truth of a belief, the threshold question of whether it was "truly held" could be resolved by the courts.[46]

The status of the conscientious objector was extended further in *Welsh v. United States* to include the realm of "religious belief" by "all those whose consciences spurred by deeply held moral, ethical, or religious beliefs would give them no rest or peace if they allowed themselves to become a part of an instrument of war."[47] Thus, in the context of counseling malpractice cases, the only issue that the courts could properly review is whether the counsel of the counselor was indeed a belief held in good faith.

The Supreme Court has also examined first amendment rights in determining whether a tort has been committed. In *New York Times Co. v. Sullivan*,[48] a public official sought to recover damages for a defamatory falsehood published in the *New York Times* relating to his official conduct. In reversing the Alabama courts' decisions, the Supreme Court held that the Alabama courts failed to safeguard the first amendment freedoms of speech and press.[49] The Court then imposed a burden of proving that the "statement was made with 'actual malice' —that is, with knowledge that it was false or with reckless disregard of whether it was false or not."[50] The Court stated that the first amendment protects erroneous speech about public officials, which might otherwise be defamation if it referred to private citizens, because of the need for "breathing space" for the freedom of expression to survive.[51]

By analogy, the free exercise clause, which has been called the "favored child of the First Amendment,"[52] should receive similar safeguards. The "actual malice" standard may be an even more rigid standard than the "sincerity" test of *Ballard*. Arguably, the protection offered spiritual counselors should be greater than the protection given the press in their coverage of public officials since the public official would not have control over the publicity generated by the media. In counseling cases, however, it is the counselee who voluntarily seeks out the counselor and is free to accept or reject the counseling given.

Arguably, counseling by religious groups and clergy that is shown to be malicious should not receive first amendment protection. A narrow "actual malice" test may avoid first amendment obstacles. The failure of a spiritual counselor to embrace either the views or "treatment" preferred by the vast majority of professionals would not render him or her liable unless "actual malice" was proven.

This approach would be consistent with the most recent Supreme Court decision on the protection offered individuals whose point of view differs from the majority in the moral or religious sphere. In *Wooley v. Maynard,*[53] the Supreme Court held that a Jehovah's Witness could not be punished by the State of New Hampshire for covering up the state motto "live free or die" on his automobile license plates—a motto that he considered repugnant to his moral, religious, and political beliefs. Chief Justice Burger, writing for the Court, noted that the individual was forced to express "an ideological point of view" he could not accept.[54]

> The First Amendment protects the right of individuals to hold a point of view different from the majority and to refuse to foster, in the way New Hampshire commands, an idea they find morally objectionable.[55]

Inevitably, there will be times when the counsel given by a clergyperson of one sect will appear to be "morally objectionable" and even "repugnant" to the moral and religious beliefs of the majority. It is when the courts undertake the task of selecting one system of belief for preferred treatment that the first amendment is violated.

In *Rosicrucian Fellowship v. Rosicrucian Nonsectarian Church*[56] the California Supreme Court provided a helpful summary of the types of ecclesiastical matters that the courts should avoid:

> "The courts of the land are not concerned with mere polemic discussions and cannot coerce the performance of obligations of a spiritual character, or adopt a judicial standard for theological orthodoxy, or determine the abstract truth of religious doctrines, or adjudicate whether a certain person is a Catholic in good standing, or settle mere questions of faith or doctrine, or make changes in the liturgy, or dictate the policy of a church in the seating of the sexes or the playing of instrumental music, or decide who the rightful leader of a church ought to be, or enjoin a clergyman from striking the complainant's name from his register of communicants, or enforce the religious right of a member to partake of the Lord's Supper." . . . It is also settled principle that: "It is perfectly clear that whatever church relationship is maintained in the United States is not a matter of status. It is based not on residence, or birth, or compulsion but on voluntary consent. It rests on faith, 'primarily, faith in God and his teachings; secondarily, faith in and reliance upon each other.' It is 'one of contract.' and is therefore exactly what the parties to it make it and nothing

more. A person who joins a church covenants expressly or impliedly that in consideration of the benefits which result from such a union he [or she] will submit to its control and be governed by its laws, usages, and customs whether they are of an ecclesiastical or temporal character to which laws, usages, and customs [s]he assents as to so many stipulations of a contract."[57]

Clearly, counseling offered by the clergy touches on a number of these areas.

Conclusion

The law of torts has been the battleground for social theory. Each new theory raises far more questions than answers, and the theory of clergy malpractice is no exception. Since clergy malpractice inevitably deals with doctrinal, ecclesiastical, and spiritual issues, judicial review will force the courts into dangerous territory. Thus, with the possible exception of the instance where "actual malice" on the part of the counselor is alleged to exist, it seems clear that the first amendment will bar the introduction of this theory into the legal arena.

II. Is the Cloth Unraveling?
A First Look at Clergy Malpractice

Ben Zion Bergman

With the proliferation of malpractice suits against physicians, surgeons, lawyers, dentists, psychiatrists, and psychologists, it may be only natural for all professionals to see the specter of malpractice lurking in the not too distant shadows. Insurance companies have been greatly affected by the phenomenon.[1] Malpractice suits with their attendant judgments often border on the astronomical.

Some insurance companies have even begun to write malpractice policies for clergymen.[2] An article in *Liberty Magazine,*[3] later excerpted in *Trial,*[4] investigated the advertising claims of these insurance companies which cited case histories of clergymen being sued by disgruntled parishioners. The article concludes that the prospect of clergy malpractice suits may be an invention of insurance companies. As of this writing, however, a suit has been filed in the California Superior Court for the

County of Los Angeles in which the complaint specifically alleged "Clergyman Malpractice."[5] The complaint alleged that
the pastor in his role as spiritual counselor actively dissuaded
and discouraged the disturbed parishioner from continuing professional psychiatric counseling and persuaded him to confine
his psychological therapy to counseling by the minister and lay
counselors of the church, along with a regimen of prayer and
scriptural reading.[6] The young man had been recently released
from a hospital after having attempted suicide, and this fact
was known to the minister. The suit was brought by the parents
of the parishioner alleging that his subsequent suicide was the
result of the minister's advice and counsel.[7]

This is a case of first impression which raises a number of
interesting issues. Beyond the tort questions of causation and
the imposition of liability in the case of suicide, there are constitutional issues raised, the resolution of which may well require
reexamination of the first amendment's separation of church
and state.

Stated broadly, can any suit for clergy malpractice be sustained since it places the court in the position of having to pass
judgment on competence, training, methods, content, and other
aspects of the clergyman's functions? Furthermore, does not a
complaint of malpractice presume a definable duty which the
practitioner (in this case, the clergyman) has violated? Can that
duty be defined by a body other than the religious order which
has ordained and/or which the clergyman serves? In other
words, if the court were to determine the scope of the clergy's
duty of care, would that determination not be in violation of the
first amendment? Does the concept of religious liberty require
that the clergy not be regulated at all in their functions, or can
one differentiate between the purely ecclesiastical functions of
the clergy and those functions, albeit traditionally within the
clergyman's purview, that are not sacerdotal in character and
which might therefore be legitimately regulated by the court
under the police power of the state to protect the health, safety,
morals, and welfare of its citizens? Does the traditional priest-
penitent privilege militate against clergy malpractice liability?

These and other questions are basic issues which will have to
be dealt with to determine whether a suit for malpractice may
or may not be brought against a clergyman. This essay attempts
to deal with those questions which immediately surface in connection with clergy malpractice. While it will doubtlessly not be
the last word on the subject, it may very well be the first.

The Inner Tension of the First Amendment

In their desire to eliminate the abuses that the combination of spiritual and temporal power had wreaked throughout European history, and recognizing that such an "unholy alliance" could threaten the democratic foundations upon which the new republic was being established, the founding fathers in the first amendment to the Constitution enacted that "Congress shall make no law respecting the establishment of religion or prohibiting the free exercise thereof."[8] The two clauses, each of which has a laudable purpose in consonance with the requirements of the democratic order, create a tension when taken together, because the satisfaction of one may conflict with the other. If the establishment clause be regarded as forbidding any governmental aid to religion, could that not act to discriminate against and retard the free exercise of religion? If public property is available for a wide range of activities, including speakers on political and social issues, but forbidden to religious activity, does that law not impede the free exercise of religion? On the other hand, if public property is made available for religious worship and/or proselytization, isn't the government's extension of aid to religion outlawed by the establishment clause? The exemption from taxation of churches and church property is certainly governmental assistance to religious institutions. However, the recognition that "the power to tax involves the power to destroy"[9] may possibly warrant freedom from taxation as necessary for the free exercise of religion. Perhaps the clearest example of government aid to religion is providing chaplains for the armed forces.[10]

This tension between the two requirements of the first amendment lies at the heart of the difficulty in defining the amendment's scope and applicability. Thomas Jefferson defined the first amendment as "building a wall of separation between Church and State,"[11] implying that the government has no jurisdiction over religion or religious institutions, nor can it do anything to encourage religion. Jefferson's interpretation resolves the tension in favor of absolute neutrality. The other end of the spectrum is represented by Justice Joseph Story, who, by placing emphasis on the free exercise clause, understood the first amendment to be supportive of religion. Story thought the effect of the establishment clause was limited to preventing the government from giving advantage or preference to one sect or denomination, which would result in bestowing upon "a hierarchy the exclusive patronage of the national government."[12]

Traditionally, Jefferson's image of a wall of separation between church and state has been the dominant view. This view was adopted by Justice Hugo Black for the Court in *Everson v. Board of Education.*[13] While citing it favorably, Black pointed out the tension between the establishment and free exercise clauses and concluded that it was permissible for a New Jersey school district to reimburse parents for the cost of sending their children to school on the public transportation system, including transportation of some children to Catholic parochial schools, as long as the permissive statute was not discriminatory. Thus, Jefferson has been made to reconcile with Story. Small wonder that Justice Jackson, in his vigorous dissent, characterized the opinion as reminiscent of "Julia, who according to Byron's reports, whispering, 'I will ne'er consent'—consented."[14]

Maintaining the neutrality of the state toward religious activities means drawing a fine line, on one side of which the state is using its power and resources to aid the religious establishment and on the other side of which the state becomes an adversary of religion. The difficulty of drawing this line is exemplified in *Zorach v. Clauson,*[15] where the Court permitted New York City to dismiss students early for "released-time" religious instruction, distinguishing this case from an earlier decision[16] simply on the basis that in the previous case, public school classrooms were used, whereas in the present case, religious instruction was not on public school property. Justice Jackson, in his dissent, termed this distinction "trivial, almost to the point of cynicism."[17] Even Justice Black, who allowed government aid to religion in *Everson,* dissented in this case, finding that any form of release-time was "manipulating the city's compulsory education laws to help religious sects get pupils."[18]

The shortest distance between the two points of the establishment and the free exercise clauses is, therefore, a fine line but evidently not a straight one, Euclid notwithstanding.

The Clergy and the State

The difficulty of establishing the definable limits of church-state separation is reflected in the statutory exemption of clergy from government regulation or licensing. Were the state to require licensing of the clergy, it would, on the one hand, have to establish criteria of eligibility which would necessitate the state's involvement in doctrinal and theological matters clearly forbidden by the first amendment, one purpose of which was to free religious institutions from domination or interference by the state. The U.S. Supreme Court, in a number of decisions, has recognized the sacrosanct nature of theological doctrine and the exclusive right of the religious authorities to determine it.[19] On the other hand, licensing by the state, even without fixed eligibility criteria, would have the state place its imprimatur on religion and put it in the business of legitimizing anyone who claimed to be a qualified clergyman.

As a result, most states have gone to great lengths to explicitly exempt the clergy from any state regulation. For example, the California Business and Professions Code, section dealing with the licensing of physicians and surgeons, explicitly states that the provisions do not "regulate, prohibit or apply to any kind of treatment by prayer, nor interfere in any way with the practice of religion."[20]

The code section pertaining to the licensing of psychiatrists and psychiatric personnel similarly exempts from its regulations the "provision of services . . . when done by the tenets of any well-recognized church or denomination."[21]

A similar exemption is embodied in the provision regulating the licensing of marriage, family, and child counselors. The code states that "[t]he provisions of this chapter shall not apply to any priest, rabbi, or minister of the gospel of any religious denomination when performing counseling services as part of his pastoral or professional duties."[22] It should, however, be pointed out that a distinction is made between the clergyman's counseling function "as part of his pastoral or professional duties"—performed as part of his congregational responsibilities—and the clergyman seeking to serve as a private marriage, family, and child counselor, apart from church-connected activity. In the latter case, licensing is required, and the regulations of the code apply despite the religious orientation or ecclesiastical ordination of the counselor. In fact, the trend has been to tighten the requirements in this regard. This is reflected in the 1981 amendment of section 17804[23] of the California Business and Professions Code, which sets out the educational and experiential qualifications for licensing as a marriage, family, and child counselor. The original section 17804(b)[24] required two years' experience of an acceptable type, the acceptability of which was at the discretion of the director of the licensing agency. Since there is a reverential attitude toward clergy that makes it difficult to say no to them, and failure to accept the applicant's experience gleaned during years in the ministry could be viewed as disparaging of religion, a clergy applicant was invariably credited with the requisite experience as long as he had served in the ministry for at least two years. The amended section 17804(c)[25] requires that the experience has been gained under the supervision of a licensed marriage, family, or child counselor, or certain other licensed persons such as psychiatrists or psychologists. This would eliminate automatic experience credit for pastors, even if they had worked under and been supervised by a senior pastor of the church, since that senior pastor would not necessarily have been a licensed counselor.[26] Amended section 17804(a) imposes stricter educational requirements.[27] The California Administrative Code similarly reflects these more stringent requirements, both in the area of education and experience.[28]

An even more graphic example is that of the *mohel,* which is the term denoting the performer of Jewish ritual circumcision. A search of the codes of those states with the largest Jewish populations[29] reveals that none requires that a *mohel* be licensed. Presumably this is so because the *mohel* is a religious functionary—indeed, many if not most of them have rabbinical ordination—and the state will not interfere with or attempt to regulate this religious practice. Yet it is entirely conceivable that if the *mohel* were to perform a circumcision on a non-Jewish child or adult, not as part of a religious rite, he would be guilty of practicing medicine without a license.

The reluctance, therefore, of the state to regulate the activities of the clergyman relates to his duties as a religious functionary. The same function outside the ecclesiastical office is subject to regulation and licensing by the state.

A Sword or a Shield

The protection that the clergy enjoys from governmental interference is clearly limited to ministerial functions performed in the course of the clergyman's ecclesiastical office. The extent of that protection may, in turn, depend on the scope allotted to the ecclesiastical office. It is certain that any complaint arising out of a purely sacerdotal act of the minister would not be actionable. No one can sue a minister, alleging that the complainant's decedent did not get to heaven because the minister did not perform the funeral service properly. Outside of problems of proof, the court would be involved in judging both doctrine and ritual. Nor could a priest be sued for alleged malpractice in the baptismal rite. It would be equally unacceptable to allow a suit in which a rabbi is charged with improper performance of a Bar Mitzvah. Even if damages could be assessed in these cases (a highly improbable supposition), the very fact that the court would have to rule on matters of doctrine and ritual that the first amendment removes from the Court's jurisdiction makes such a suit untenable.

There are, however, functions the clergyman may perform in the course of his ministerial duties that are not directly ecclesiastical in nature but may be ancillary to such an ecclesiastical function. It could be argued that almost every waking hour of the clergyman's day is spent in pursuit of his pastoral duties, but would that necessarily free him from any liability for a tort committed in the course of fulfillment of those duties? If while driving to the hospital to visit and pray with a sick parishioner the pastor is involved in a traffic accident, is he *ipso facto* immune from liability merely because he was engaged in a pastoral function?

In a suit brought in California against a church and its ministers for damages resulting from an automobile accident which occurred when the minister was driving children to the congregation's Bible school, Justice Traynor declared that the public policy expressed in the Civil Code that everyone is responsible for the result of his acts, both willful and negligent "admits of no exception based upon the objectives, however laudable, of the tortfeasor."[30] To rule otherwise would be tantamount to arguing that a clergyman should be exempt from the requirement of obtaining a driver's license, since he needs to drive in the performance of his functions and requiring a license inhibits the free exercise of religion. Such an argument cannot prevail against the state's right and duty to safeguard the lives and property of its citizens by imposing testing and licensing requirements upon all drivers, regardless of their religious activities.

The courts have not hesitated to impose civil liability upon churches and religious organizations, maintaining that such liability does not conflict with the free exercise clause of the first amendment. In *Barr v. United Methodist Church*,[31] the court distinguished between the freedom to believe and the freedom to act, maintaining that conduct, albeit based upon religious motivations, is subject to regulation and restriction for the protection of society.[32] The alternative would be anarchic and would result in making "the professed doctrine's religious belief superior to the law of the land and, in effect, to permit every citizen to become a law unto himself. Government could exist in name only under such circumstances."[33]

The first amendment, under certain circumstances, may be a shield. But broadening its scope to clothe religious organizations and clergy with blanket immunity from prosecution could transform it into a sword.

The above are examples of situations in which the conduct complained of was ancillary to the religious function. It was not necessary for the courts to make a determination regarding ecclesiastical doctrine. Yet, as we move closer to issues involving such determinations, we find cases in which the court has subjected those issues to judicial scrutiny.[34] The California Business and Professions Code specifies, as a qualification for regulatory exemption, that the exempt religious body be a *"well-recognized church or denomination."* [35] This criterion is relative, and administration of the code provision requires a determination as to the recognized legitimacy of the religious organization in question. However, such a determination places the state in the position of making a determination not only regarding the organization seeking the exemption from governmental regulation but the legitimacy of the religion itself. It is platitudinous to point out that Jesus and Mohammed were heretics in their day. Paul and the early Christians did not comprise a "well-recognized church or denomination," but the history of religion is replete with examples of the heresy of yesterday becoming the orthodoxy of today. Is it therefore at all legitimate for the government even to inquire into the legitimacy of the religious sect, its doctrines, and its proponents? If the answer is no, the door then is open to anyone claiming ministerial status and first amendment protection merely by alleging to be the recipient of a new revelation.

Such was the case of *Theriault v. Carlson,*[36] in which a prisoner claimed first amendment protection for his new religion (which he called the Eccletarian Faith) embodied in what he called "the Church of the New Song." The court, while admitting the difficulty of establishing standards and criteria by which to judge the legitimacy of a religion, nevertheless stated that "such difficulties have proved to be of no hindrance to denials of First Amendment protection to so-called religions which tend to mock established institutions and are obviously shams and absurdities and whose members are patently devoid of religious sincerity."[37] This might be termed audacious or arrogant and even fraught with danger. Would Jesus, Mohammed, and Luther have passed the test? Didn't they, as well as Abraham, whom Jewish legend credits with breaking his father's idols, "mock established institutions"? Perhaps the crucial element is "religious sincerity." But isn't that, at best, a subjective evaluation, and how is it proved, short of martyrdom, at which point the issue becomes moot? Furthermore, when "mail order" ordination is available, isn't such a determination necessary to protect the public, the taxpayer, and the government itself from fraud? We are, therefore, regrettably faced with the ineluctable conclusion that such judicial inquiry may sometimes be both legitimate and necessary, albeit to be exercised with great caution. The court can only exercise the judgment of today, leaving the verdict of history to ratify or reject.

Establishing standards of competence and performance for religious institutions and their functionaries, with the imposition of liability for their breach, will involve the court in questions that touch tangentially on matters of religious doctrine and practice. Without more, this is insufficient to make the imposition of those standards a violation of the free exercise clause.

Even if the legitimacy of the religious body is not in question, the protection of third parties, the public, and the very institutions of government itself may outweigh any claim to first amendment protection. In *United States v. Speers*,[38] the contention that as a Black Muslim he used marijuana and peyote in religious rites did not avail the defendant, who was convicted of smuggling those drugs. The public policy militating against the use of and traffic in those drugs was sufficiently strong to deny constitutional privilege to their use in religious ceremonies. In another case the danger of the public's exposure to communicable disease and concern for the child's welfare outweighed a father's claim that compulsory vaccination was in violation of his religious beliefs.[39] The same considerations held true in the famous case of *Jehovah's Witnesses in the State of Washington v. Kings County Hospital*,[40] which upheld a judge's right to order blood transfusions for a child despite the fact that blood transfusions were violations of the parents' religious beliefs. In a related case,[41] the court would not allow the Federal Food, Drug, and Cosmetic Act to be violated or even suspended to allow the importation of a device which the church claimed was used in its confessional practices.

These and other cases point to the fact that freedom of religion cannot be used to subvert the state's legitimate police power. Nor can freedom of religion be used to escape liability to innocent third parties or to the public. This would permit religious functionaries to commit the most egregious acts with impunity.

The Secularization of Clergy Functions

The preceding discussion, which was necessary to show that the first amendment does not clothe religious bodies and their personnel with total immunity from governmental scrutiny and regulation, still does not touch the issue of clergy malpractice. While it is clear that injury resulting to third parties or the public from the clergyman's nonecclesiastical acts will impose liability, that is a far cry from saying that the clergy must adhere to certain standards of competence and performance in the execution of their ministerial functions and that failure to abide by these standards may make them liable for the consequences to the recipients of their ministrations.

The concept of clergy malpractice goes further by imposing liability, not for some tangential consequence but for failure to execute the ministerial duty properly. The question at issue is whether the execution of the ministerial function itself can be tortiously performed.

As indicated previously, the purely sacerdotal functions of the clergy are immune from attack. The congregant may not like the rabbi's sermon, the cantor's chanting, the priest's intonation of the mass, or the minister's method of sprinkling the water in the baptism—may even feel injured thereby—but no court would arrogate to itself the right to establish standards of proper performance in these matters. These are uniquely sacerdotal functions not performed by anyone other than the clergy. There are, therefore, no external guidelines by which to measure competence, and the imposition of standards by the court would be a direct interference with religious functions, which is expressly prohibited by the first amendment.

There are functions, however, which are not unique to the clergy, even though they may be traditionally part of the clergy's role and possibly even originated within a religious context. A prime example of this is the counseling role. The question is, therefore, whether the religious practitioner can be held to a standard of duty when a secular practitioner is so held.

In *McGowan v. Maryland*,[42] which upheld Maryland's statute mandating Sunday closing for certain businesses and exempting others, Chief Justice Warren, speaking for the Court, freely acknowledged the religious origin of Sunday closing laws. He traced the history of these laws from medieval English statutes through their continuation and further development in colonial America and concluded that the Sunday legislation was in aid of the established church.[43] The opinion then traced the secularization of Sunday closing and its justification on other than religious grounds—for example, the protection of labor, and providing a day for family activity—resulting in "the evolution of Sunday laws as temporal statutes."[44] Thus when activities that originated in a religious context and were motivated by religious doctrine become secularized, their religious origin becomes irrelevant.

The secularization of the Sunday abstinence from regular acts of labor finds a parallel in the secularization of other activities that had their origins in the religious functions of the clergy. There is no question that it was the clergyman who filled the role of spiritual adviser, counseling his congregants on matters that disturbed them. In medieval Europe, where the priest may have been the only educated or literate person in the community, his counsel was sought on matters pragmatic as well as spiritual. He was the one who sought to help his parishioners achieve the mental and emotional equilibrium to enable them to cope with the problems of life and its stresses. With the expansion of knowledge and the advent of scientific inquiry, which so greatly enhanced man's understanding of himself and his world, some of these functions were taken over by laymen who acquired special competence in these areas. Just as the witch doctor's role was taken over by the physician, so the field of emotional and psychological counseling was secularized when non-clerics acquired special understanding of human behavior and expertise in dealing with its problems and aberrations. Knowledge in this area has expanded to the point where it has become a separate academic discipline. As a result, competence, which is directly proportional to the body of knowledge, has become more and more dependent on special training and education. While an individual may possess a measure of intuitive skill and competence, that by itself is no longer reliable in light of our greater understanding of the complexity of the human personality. The recognition of this fact by the clergy themselves has resulted in courses in pastoral psychology as part of the regular curriculum in many, if not most, seminaries. These courses are most often taught by psychiatrists or psychologists whose special training was acquired under secular auspices. In more fundamentalist seminaries the instructor may be an experienced pastor with special skills.

The creation of a separate academic discipline and training has also resulted in the creation of a profession with standards of proper and improper techniques, methods, and procedures. The lay practitioner is held responsible for adherence to what are considered normative procedures by the profession, with resultant liability for injury caused by breach of those professional standards. Is there any reason why the clergy-practitioner should not also be held accountable for certain minimal standards, which may not necessarily be identical with those required by the more highly trained professional? With the secularization of the counseling function, it can conceptually be separable from the clergy's ecclesiastic or purely religious function, and the imposition of a duty of care and competence could be considered not violative of first amendment strictures against governmental interference with the free exercise of religion.

Duty Defined by State of the Art

The secularization of certain areas of the clergy's functions, therefore, removes those areas from being uniquely the clergyman's province, even though the clergyman still continues to view them as incumbent upon him by virtue of his religious office and may even approach his function in those areas with some different suppositions and different techniques from the non-clerical practitioner. Nevertheless, the fact that others than members of the clergy are engaged in the same general activity makes that activity amenable to scrutiny and evaluation by other than ecclesiastical authorities. The secular professional becomes subject to a duty to adhere to professional standards with liability for damage resulting from their violation. That duty is not a constant. It evolves with the state of the art and with the growth of knowledge and scientific certainty. To the extent that certain procedures, standards, techniques, and scientific truths, for example, become accepted and acknowledged by the professional community, the greater the liability of the individual practitioner for their neglect, misapplication, or incompetent administration. The physician is not required to administer every diagnostic test possible to every patient. But if the consensus of the medical community is that a confluence of certain symptoms points to the possibility of a certain disease or physical disorder, ascertainable by a specific test, then failure to administer that test would be malfeasance on the part of the physician, with malpractice liability for any injurious results.

While the validity of various counseling techniques or certain psychiatric or psychological theories may be debatable, no one can deny that the science of psychology has made important discoveries, has established certain minimal truths about human behavior, has effectively categorized mental disorders, and has developed accepted diagnostic and therapeutic techniques. The measure of a psychiatrist's competence cannot now be defined within strict parameters: "To date, psychiatry has not clearly defined the skills [the psychiatrist] must demonstrate in order to be certified as competent. It is our belief that the profession can no longer avoid beginning the difficult, often emotion-laden task of specifying what a psychiatrist should know and be able to do."[45]

While this passage expresses dissatisfaction with the present lack of definition of competence, the authors, nevertheless, are voicing their belief that it is possible to define it, arduous as the task may be. This means that there is presently a body of recognized and accepted knowledge and skills sufficiently acknowledged to be considered fundamental to a psychiatrist's competence, albeit not sufficiently spelled out.

In an even earlier article, this assumption that the state of the art is such that duty can be implied is manifested by the authors when they delineate some twelve areas potentially subject to psychiatric malpractice.[46]

Such being the case, should the clergyman, who holds himself and his services out to the community as a counselor competent to deal with emotional problems, not be subject to some minimal level of competence in the art of science of therapeutic counseling, as determined or gauged by the state of the science or art? May the clergyman practice his counseling with total disregard of the scientific advances made in that area?

To make the point even more forcefully, let us return to the graphic example of the *mohel*. The practice of ritual circumcision originated in antiquity and its rules were developed before the discovery of microscopic organisms and their relation to infection. If a *mohel* today were to perform a circumcision in the same manner as it was performed two thousand years ago, without sterilizing his instruments, and if infection were to result, would we not be justified in considering him to have breached a duty of care? Can he be allowed to act, oblivious of the universally recognized knowledge of modern antisepsis? To compound the example, in Talmudic times it was considered a mandatory procedure for the *mohel* to suck out some of the blood from the incision.[47] Today's medical knowledge was unknown and the danger of infection unrealized. Indeed, it is precisely because of the medical knowledge of the day that such an act was considered hygienically beneficial and therefore mandated by the religious law. A *mohel* who failed to do so was removed and replaced. A modern *mohel* who wishes to conform to the religious law, not content with merely soaking up some blood with absorbent cotton, uses a pipette device, so that his mouth does not come in contact with the open incision. This removes the danger of infection from his germ-laden mouth. But what if the *mohel* today were to insist that as a matter of religious conscience he must perform the act by mouth as specified in the Talmud? Could we justifiably exonerate him from any liability for resultant infection?

The *mohel*'s lay counterparts, the physicians or surgeons who perform circumcision, would be liable for malpractice were they to perform a circumcision in such a manner. In *Valentine v. Kaiser Foundation Hospitals,*[48] a medical malpractice action arising out of a circumcision performed on the minor plaintiff, the doctor and the hospital were held liable for the grievous harm sustained as a result of subsequent infection. Would there be any justification in holding the physician liable and the *mohel* innocent if both violated an elemental and universally known medical principle, known to the *mohel* no less than to the physician? This would permit the first amendment to be used as a shield in a manner never intended. Similarly, clergy counselors should be liable for the tortious results of their acts if the acts violate elemental psychological knowledge. One could even argue that religious conscience would impel members of the clergy to acquire a greater measure of competence and responsibility in order to serve their congregants more capably. Unfortunately, this is not always the case. The imposition of liability, far from exerting a chilling effect upon the clergy-congregant relationship, would enhance it by giving congregants a greater sense of security in the clergy's competence and sincerity.

Both considerations of justice for the victim of incompetence and the enhancement of the clergy's effectiveness would seem to militate in favor of clergy liability.

Setting the Standards

Liability for malpractice requires establishment of minimal standards of performance to which the clergy can reasonably be expected to conform. These standards cannot be created *ex nihilo* but will be the product of an evolutionary process. Once clergy malpractice becomes accepted as a cause of action, duty patterns will begin to emerge through court decisions.

Where the clergy's function is a prescribed physical act, such as sterile techniques for the *mohel,* it will be relatively easy to set duties. Where the clergy's role does not require specific physical acts, such as counseling, the problem is much more difficult.

The same level of competence and professional knowledge cannot be expected from the clergy as can be expected from the psychiatrist, whose education and training is more intensively specialized. Therefore, the duty cannot be the same. However, by virtue of the unique relationship between minister and congregant, there are situations where he can be more effective than the psychiatrist or psychologist. Milton Malev writes:

> The minister of religion possesses in his person and his position a unique armamentarium for dealing with many facets of human distress. He carries a symbolic meaning which, properly utilized, has the power to ease fear, lighten guilt, resolve perplexity, disarm anger, lift despair and give renewed meaning to life in one whose life has ceased to have meaning. He applies reason and exhortation, gives instruction and guidance, exercises authority, receives confession and offers prayer. These measures bring relief and comfort to the wounded in spirit.
>
> There are, however, people in whom these same painful emotions, superficially indistinguishable, are the product of mental disorder and hence not accessible to these tools of the ministers. ... They require the care of a physician and failure to recognize these disorders may lead to difficulties for congregant and minister alike.[49]

It is in the latter part of the above statement that we may find a starting point for a clergyman's duty as a counselor. In an article entitled "Avoiding Psychiatric Malpractice."[50] among the areas of potential malpractice the authors list failure to diagnose properly and failure to consult a specialist. The California Association of Marriage and Family Counselors lists as a duty of its members: "The Marriage and Family counselor recognizes the boundaries of one's competence and the limitation of one's techniques. The Marriage and Family Counselor assists his/her client in obtaining appropriate professional help for aspects of the person's problems that fall outside the MFCC's individual competence."[51]

We can possibly compare the relationship of clergy and professional psychiatrist or psychologist to that of general practitioner and specialist. Just as the medical general practitioner has the duty to call in a specialist if a reasonably careful general practitioner would do so under the circumstances, so the first duty of clergy should be to recognize when the problem is beyond their skill and refer the congregant to one with more specialized training.

There are two aspects to this. The first is the ability to diagnose the more obvious types of mental disorders, or at least the ability to discern when the counselee's problem is of a magnitude beyond the counselor's skills and ability. This is a duty of competence. The corollary duty to refer the counselee to a more competent person when the clergy counselor is beyond his depth is an ethical duty. A practicing counseling psychologist and university professor writes:

> As a basic ethical principle, therapists are expected to recognize the boundaries of their competence and their own personal and professional limitations. Ethical therapists do not employ diagnostic or treatment procedures that are beyond the scope of their training, nor do they accept clients whose personal functioning is seriously impaired, unless they are qualified to work with those clients. A therapist who becomes aware of his or her lack of competence in a particular case has the responsibility to seek consultation with colleagues or with a supervisor or to make a referral.[52]

Characterizing this duty as an ethical obligation makes it imposable upon the clergy, from whom, if from no one else, one has a reasonable expectation of ethical behavior.

This is understandably a change from the traditional role of the clergy, who by reason of the special sanctity attached to their person and function and by virtue of being viewed as one in a specially intimate relationship with God, have tended to regard themselves and be regarded by others as a source of final authority. The mere force of tradition, however, is inadequate to withstand the modern realities created by greater scientific knowledge. No one would seriously consider allowing barbers today to act as healers through bloodletting, although that was once their traditional function. While that example is more extreme than our clergy counselor case, the two are analogous.

This duty, however, does not totally deprive the clergy of their function as counselor. There are people who need psychiatric help, and people who need religious counseling. The practitioners in each field make efforts to recognize the others' field of usefulness and to make it available to the people who come to them for help.[53]

Imposing this duty upon the clergy does not make them mere referral agencies for the secular professional. It is a duty that derives from their obligation to expand their own usefulness and provide more valuable service to their people. While this duty cannot be imposed upon a friendly neighbor to whom one might turn for advice, it is imposable upon the clergy, who hold themselves out as possessing a degree of expertise and, who, by virtue of their position, tacitly invite solicitation of their counsel.

The Clergy-Penitent Privilege

The privilege of maintaining and enforcing the confidentiality of communications between clergy and penitent is sanctified by history and enshrined by codification.[54] It has been argued that imposition of malpractice liability would undermine the clergy-penitent privilege.[55] The argument is made that if liability may lie for clergy malpractice, the church and the minister would have to protect themselves through insurance. Since the insured has a duty to cooperate with the insurer in defending a lawsuit,[56] the clergy would be put in the position of having to testify and disclose the content of the privileged communication, thus vitiating the privilege. Concomitantly, the penitent could not rely on the privilege and therefore could not be entirely open and honest, which in turn would impair the quality and value of the counseling.[57]

This argument is specious for a number of reasons. First, such an argument could be raised in any cause of action for professional malpractice in which privilege exists between the professional and the client, be it doctor-patient or attorney-client. In those instances, too, the professional is protected from liability by insurance. Yet this has not destroyed the privilege or its effectiveness. Second, the argument fails to deal with the realities of the situation. The clergy-penitent privilege is dual; it can be invoked by either party when testimony is solicited by a third party. When clergy are sued for malpractice by penitents, the latter have impliedly waived their privilege. It would be incongruous to deny the clergy, or any other privileged professionals, the right to defend themselves by allowing opponents to invoke the privilege.

Summary and Conclusion

The question of clergy malpractice raises thorny and complicated first amendment issues relative to church-state separation. The tension between the establishment clause and the free exercise clause makes it difficult to draw the line with any certitude between permissible and impermissible state intervention in religious functions. While the clergy have been exempt from regulation and licensing, in contradistinction to other professionals, the courts have not hesitated to exercise jurisdiction in those cases where the court's scrutiny impinged tangentially on matters of doctrine and belief. First amendment protection is not absolute and inviolate but is subject to being outweighed by the state's duty to protect its citizens. The clergy's first amendment protection, therefore, cannot be used to subvert the state's duty. Furthermore, the amendment, as expressed in state codes, has been construed as limiting its protection to the purely ecclesiastical and sacerdotal functions of the clergy. Some of these traditional functions have become secularized, and the secular practitioners have become subject to standards of conduct and duties of care. Furthermore, the expansion of scientific knowledge in these areas necessitates that the practitioner have some minimum measure of education and training and cannot rely on intuition or native ability alone. This should hold true in some degree for the clergy, who should not be allowed to function in disregard of established principles. The minimal duty which at the outset can and should be imposed upon the clergy is to recognize their own limitations and to refer those cases which are beyond their competence to practitioners with more specialized training. Breach of this duty would subject clergy to suit for malpractice. This is an ethical duty, and the imposition of liability, far from denigrating the position and efficaciousness of the clergy, would enhance it. Nor would such liability adversely affect the clergy-penitent relationship or its privilege.

The Talmud says that with the destruction of the Holy Temple in Jerusalem the gift of prophecy was taken from the prophets and given to fools. I, nevertheless, will run the risk of being considered a fool by prophesying that even if the concept of clergy malpractice becomes recognized by the courts as a valid cause of action, it will not result in a sudden torrent of clergy malpractice cases. Most people have an inherent respect for the clergy and share the feeling that to sue them partakes of irreverence, which sentiment would act as a deterrent to bringing suit. As a member of the clergy, I am selfishly in accord with that sentiment.

3

Pastoral Accountability in the Bible and Theology

Samuel Southard

In the May 1922 issue of the *Annals of the American Academy of Political and Social Science,* S. Z. Batten wrote on "The Ethics of the Ministry." This was one in a series of articles on professional ethics, but Batten did not consider the ministry to be a profession. Rather, he saw it as a "calling." The will of God was expected to be the dominant motive for pastoral service. Because of the spiritual nature of the pastoral office, the author did not see any need for a professional code of ethics. The church expected the clergy to live ethically, and this requirement should be enough to enforce ethical accountability.

Why have clergy been content to practice their calling without a prescribed code of ethics, and why has society been willing for churches to hold clergy accountable for ethical behavior without prescribed codes? Bearing in mind the threat of malpractice suits in the 1980s, we will examine four questions: What is the basic authority of the clergy to practice their calling or profession? What are the criteria by which a clergy person is considered competent to perform his or her calling? What specific functions of the clergy must be examined for possible consequences of malpractice? What special responsibility do the clergy have as representatives of religion in a conversation with troubled people? This last question is aimed at the traditional understanding of "the seal of the confessional" or "the right to silence," which is occasionally questioned by civil and criminal courts.

Biblical Authority for Pastoral Practice

A definition of pastoral authority will reduce the dangers of malpractice in two ways. First, clergy who practice within the range of their authority are less liable than those who extend their practice into other fields. For example, the practice of "spiritual direction" is clearly within the confines of pastoral duties and has never been cause for liability. On the other hand, a pastor might be held liable for claiming to be a psychologist or psychiatrist. In the suit against Grace Community Church, attorneys for the parents of the young man who committed suicide were of the opinion that people in the church "are offering counseling to very sick people."[1]

A second protection against malpractice is the concentration of responsibility upon activities that have always been accepted as spiritual functions of the clergy. The definition of these functions and their control is a responsibility of the churches themselves (at least since the disestablishment of state support of the church in New England in the 1820s). Evidence of unethical conduct is usually first identified in the congregation, and discipline is exercised by the congregation. The *Los Angeles Times* on Saturday, May 30, 1981, concluded an article on "Affairs: Clergymen Struggling with Opportunities—and Failing," with the example of a San Marino church in which a minister confessed to adultery, resigned his pastorate, and was suspended from his pastoral duties for six months by the presbytery. There are occasional exceptions in which an irate husband hauls a pastor into a secular court. In a celebrated case of the nineteenth century, Theodore Tilton brought suit against the popular Brooklyn preacher Henry Ward Beecher. Tilton's accusations of alienation of his wife's affections were not sustained by the court, in part because the defense argued that "all the scoffers and the infidels have been trying all the Christians."[2]

This quotation from Beecher's defense highlights the spiritual source of authority for the pastor. It is contained in the words of the apostle Peter to a religious tribunal: "We must obey God rather than men" (Acts 5:29). To know and serve God is the primary authority of the pastor. This authority is essentially personal. The apostle Paul grounded his authority in his ability to suffer for the sake of the gospel (2 Cor. 11:23–28). Jesus told his disciples that "whoever would be first among you must be your slave; even as the Son of man came not to be served but to serve, and to give his life as a ransom for many" (Matt. 20:28).

In examining these and other New Testament passages, the Roman Catholic theologian John L. McKenzie concluded, "These sayings reveal a new conception of society and of authority, which must be formed not on the model of secular government but on the mission of Jesus himself."[3]

The personal authority is authenticated through loving service. Those who are accepted as authoritative ministers of Christ are those who have a fundamental concern for the lives of others without regard for themselves.[4] The emphasis is still so important that a recent survey of lay and clergy opinions concerning the ministry showed that pastors are regarded above all else as persons who serve without regard for acclaim. As for pastoral counselors, they are described more in terms of personal characteristics than skills. Counselors are to be compassionate, humble, understanding, and honest.[5]

The personal discipleship of the pastor is confirmed by the congregation and by ecclesiastical leaders. Authority then derives both from the quality of the personal life of the clergy and the ordination and installation of such a person as pastor of a congregation. Members of the early church were told to esteem those who were "over" them (1 Thess. 5:12), to obey the doctrine as taught by apostles (Rom. 16:17, 19), to "submit" to rulers of the flock as required (Heb. 13:17). At the same time, the pastors were admonished not to lord it over the flock but to be examples (1 Peter 5:3).

The combination of character with ecclesiastical authority has developed several traditional designations of legitimacy for the clergy: (1) the derived authority that the pastor has received from church and community tradition, (2) a legal responsibility to function as a representative of an established institution and to uphold the norms of that institution, (3) the charismatic hold that a saintly or heroic individual has upon listeners, and (4) the technical knowledge that a person offers without coercion to those who need spiritual help.[6]

Criteria of Competence

Because of the continued emphasis upon character, the competence of the clergy has centered more upon attitudes than upon skills. These attitudes are judged first of all by the life and command of the Lord Jesus. Those who are obedient to him through humble and sacrificial service are accounted worthy of his name (Matt. 20:20–28; John 13:1–20; 2 Cor. 7:15; Phil. 2:12; 1 Thess. 5:12–13). These marks of a genuine disciple are sufficient for the pastor as one member of the body of Christ to admonish another, to call all to suffer for one another, and to build up one another (Rom. 15:14; 1 Cor. 3:16; 2 Thess. 3:14–15; 1 Cor. 12:26; Eph. 4:12).

We should note that the New Testament emphasis is upon service by the entire body of Christ and is not limited to work performed by a pastor. For this reason, our discussion about liability in the ministry is meant not only for those who are ordained but also for those who function as lay counselors.

Some special requirements, however, are laid upon those who have received the gifts of preaching, teaching, or healing (1 Tim. 3:1–7; Titus 1:6–9). These persons, "set apart" by the church for specific service to the church, are expected to be without fault.

These qualifications do not include technical competence. They are drawn more toward the central theme of pastoral authority, which is an attitude of humble and sacrificial service according to the model of Christ.

The list of qualifications in the pastoral epistles would be qualifications for competence only in the sense that the pastor must demonstrate the "fruit of the Spirit" (Gal. 5:13), evident marks of God's Spirit in his or her life. Without spiritual fruit, there is no evidence for authority in the work of the pastor. (This was the long-drawn-out conclusion of the eighteenth-century conflict between William Tennent's "Log Cabin" Presbyterian preachers, who stressed "heartfelt" religious experiences, and the Old School devotees of the Westminster Confession as a criterion for ordination.)

The elevation of spiritual competence above all others is maintained in the modern church. In an interdenominational survey in 1967, I found that laity expect the ministry to emphasize "spiritual advice" at such times as death in the home, physical illness, family trouble, serious moral problems, or doubts about the Christian faith. In contrast, the laity would go to some other professional person if they were faced with financial need, physical or mental illness, uncertainty about work or career, or a decision about community action.[7]

The Legitimate Functions of a Pastor

Although the authority of a pastor rests more with attitudes than skills, the historical functions of the pastorate are well defined. They have been delineated by William Clebsch and Charles Jaekel as healing, sustaining, guidance, and reconciliation.[8]

Healing has been traditionally associated with visitation of the sick, prayer, and anointing with oil (James 5:14–16). In the tradition of the church, much of this healing was exercised by especially charismatic persons. In the twentieth century, this tradition has been continued, along with some additional emphasis upon psychological healing.

Potential problems with malpractice can arise when a pastor uses more of a psychological than a spiritual approach to healing. That is, the pastor may embrace theories of psychosomatic medicine and counsel more as a psychologist than as a spiritual director.

But if the pastor remains within the historic emphasis upon spiritual healing or faith healing, he or she may consider this to be the only form of healing and discourage other forms of professional help. One allegation of the suit against Grace Community Church was that the pastor and church "actively dissuaded and discouraged" Ken Nally from receiving professional psychiatric help and urging him instead to counsel with lay church counselors, read the scriptures, and listen to tape-recorded sermons. (Theoretical support for this practice is presented by Jay Adams in the first thirty pages of *Competent to Counsel*.[9])

Most pastors avoid this difficulty by cooperating with other professionals in the care of the physically and mentally ill. Whenever I see signs of illness, I recommend that my counselees seek competent psychiatric, medical, or other services in addition to those that I can provide as a spiritual director. I explain that I am not an expert in psychological or medical diagnosis and cannot accept responsibility for decisions of that kind.

The second function of a pastor within the traditional role as authority is that of *sustaining* persons in time of grief, suffering, and anxiety. The risk of malpractice is greatly reduced when the pastor concentrates upon preserving the best of a person's situation despite some loss, offers consolation that points toward the destiny of the person as a child of God, consolidates the remaining resources available to the sufferer around eternal values that will maintain satisfaction despite a deprived life, and proclaims redemption, the sense of fulfillment in life that comes from identifying with the struggles, suffering, and resurrection of Christ.

Providing *guidance* is a traditional ministerial function that confronts the difficult problem of choosing among various courses of thought or action. Before the rise of "pastoral psychology" in the 1950s, this was traditionally associated with advice-giving. Since the advice was usually restricted by the spiritual expectations of the church, liability for the pastor was minimized. In the Middle Ages, the professional security of the pastor was aided by the development of penitential manuals, books for monks and clergy who heard confession and prescribed a variety of penances that were in accord with the severity of the offense and the social status of the parishioner.[10]

Since the development of pastoral psychology, guidance has emphasized listening and has reduced advice-giving. Under the influence of client-centered theories, the liability of a pastor is reduced almost to zero because of unwillingness to do more than summarize the deeper feelings revealed by clients. In the post-Vietnam era, this passive approach was challenged by an emphasis that combines sensitivity to the feelings of individuals, attentiveness to their words and meaning, and a statement by the pastor of decisions that seem appropriate in this situation, along with guidance concerning the relationship of Christian ethics and theology to the decision that needs to be made.

The fourth aspect of pastoral functioning has been *reconciliation*. This has been traditionally defined as help to persons alienated from God and neighbor which might take the form of forgiveness or of discipline. The function of discipline has developed out of New Testament references to instruction and admonition (Rom. 15:14; 1 Cor. 4:14; 10:11; Eph. 6:4; Col. 3:16; 2 Thess. 3:15). Church discipline has been seen as corporate action by the body of Christ to correct an individual who will not listen to others and to preserve the ethical identity of the congregation (Matt. 18:15–35; Acts 5:1–4; 1 Cor. 5).

Reconciliation through consolation is described throughout the New Testament as sympathetic action in response to a cry for help (Matt. 26:53; Mark 1:40; Acts 11:23; 2 Cor. 1:3–7; Gal. 6:1–10; 2 Thess. 2:17; 2 Tim. 4:2; Heb. 4:14–16; 10:25). In his survey *A History of the Cure of Souls,* John T. McNeill found the correlation between discipline and consolation to be characteristic of pastoral care and counsel through the ages.[11]

Pastoral malpractice, judged either by the church or the law courts, would result from the diminution of either discipline or consolation. If a pastor condemns people in trouble, whether from the pulpit or in private counseling, those who suffer may be incited to take legal action. There is a danger of lawsuits in "nouthetic" schools of counseling built upon condemnation and admonition. People may interpret the absolute judgments of the pastor or Christian counselor as rejection or hostility. This is a fertile field for hostile fantasies and, finally, for action against a pastor who was supposed to be of help but actually increased the hurt.

There is less danger of legal action against a pastor who overbalances consolation and never mentions discipline, as in the "nondirective" approaches to counsel of the 1950s through the 1970s. But such an incomplete approach to counsel should be a cause for discipline by the church. Unfortunately, this is usually done in a passive rather than an active way. That is, churches and clients of passive pastors may not take action against them to remove them from office. Instead, needy people turn from such clergy to seek help from secular or spiritual authorities who are open in their guidance. The preference of most people in trouble is for a pastor who is sympathetic with their concerns but is also able to discern the cause of trouble, say what it is, and guide people to spiritual resources and to solutions for their moral and spiritual dilemmas.

Special Spiritual Responsibility

The balance of discipline and consolation has been given special emphasis in the ministry of the priest or pastor as a confessor. This is an area of legal interest because of decisions by many states to exempt a pastor from testifying in a trial when the pastor asserts that information was given under "the seal of the confessional."[12]

Although confidentiality has been a key issue in the relation of the clergy to the legal involvement of people in trouble, such as in divorce cases, the emphasis upon confidentiality is not found in the New Testament. To the contrary, the advice of the apostle James is for people to confess their sin to one another (James 5:14–16). The assumption of the verse is that several elders will be present when the person who is sick makes confession. Today, confession to several persons would immediately break the seal of the confessional in either secular or canon law. Absolute confidentiality between pastor and parishioner is required for a pastor to maintain the right to silence in a court of law.

The tradition of the early church was for public confession and public repentance. Not until the ninth century did penitential manuals counsel privacy in confession and provide penalties for the violation of secrecy.[13] The Irish Christians who had been so prominent in the development of spiritual guidance were those who recommended such privacy.[14]

Private confessions were well established by 1215, when Roman Catholicism required each of the faithful to say confession at least once a year to the parish priest, but the seal of confession was often violated. Monks often criticized parish priests for sexual solicitation of women during the confession, especially if the confessions were of a sexual nature. To remedy this, Jean Gerson recommended that the confessions of women should always be made in the presence of others.[15]

The Reformers, especially Martin Luther, considered each Christian to be a priest to every other Christian and therefore rejected the necessity of confession by parishioners to a priest. Matthew 18:15–20 was interpreted by Luther to mean that all Christians were to hear confessions from others and to absolve them. No uniform requirement of confession was made by Luther. Secrecy was assumed, but the scriptural reference for confession in *Apology for the Augsburg Confession* written by Melanchthon as a disciple of Luther used James 5:16 as a key text. The emphasis here is upon mutual confession, wrote Melanchthon, rather than private enumeration of sins to a priest.[16]

The Reformed churches, under the guidance of John Calvin, recognized the seal of confession in a synod of 1612. "Ministers are forbidden to disclose to the magistrates crimes declared by those who come to him for counsel and consolation . . . lest sinners be hindered from coming to repentance, and from making a free confession to their faults."[17]

In the Church of England, a private confession in the sixteenth century was more exceptional than regular. More emphasis was placed upon personal devotion and confession before God than in the parishioner's appearance before a priest for penance and absolution. However, those who were not satisfied with their individual conversation with God or with the general confessions made during preparation for communion were advised by the *Second Prayer Book* (1552) to make re-confession to the priest of the parish when their consciences were troubled.

The varieties of confession illustrated the Reformed emphasis, principally derived from Calvin, on confession based upon scripture rather than upon church law. The three manners were confession made secretly to God, openly before the congregation, and privately to a brother.[18]

The ancient practice of confessing sin to one another was revived among the Methodists in the "class meetings" organized by John Wesley. Bands were formed separately for married men, single men, married women, and single women. Band members, beginning with the leader, were to confess their faults and temptations and the state of their souls and then accept criticism. Twelve members were to meet weekly to "help each other and to work out their salvation."[19] The practice flourished in the American colonies and was maintained until the 1850s, when the growing sophistication of Methodists inhibited this open declaration of personal problems.[20]

The Roman Catholic emphasis upon the confessional continued to emphasize the traditional boundaries of vocal, secret, true, and integral, as in the widely accepted work of Alfonso de' Liguori, *Moral Theology* (1748).

In Roman Catholicism, the combination of biblical authority with the tradition of the church has maintained the seal of the confessional. Protestants, who base the authority of the pastor upon biblical passages and who require evidence of personal religious experience from all clergy, have maintained secrecy more as an attitude of love toward people than as a specific mandate from scripture. Protestants would depend upon an application of such general admonitions as in 2 Timothy 1:7: that God gave us "a spirit of power and love and self-control." The application in the case of confidentiality would be love for the person who has revealed a confidence, self-control in keeping information to ourselves, and power to maintain that confidence in the face of legal or other threats.

Summary

The accountability of a pastor has been primarily in the area of spiritual authority, which has been judged by the church rather than by secular courts. The nature of this authority is demonstrated in an emphasis upon the seal of the confessional, in which persons are able to unburden themselves before God in the presence of another believer and receive absolution without public disclosure.

4

Church Discipline: Handle with Care

Samuel Southard

The most neglected aspect of pastoral ministry has suddenly become headline news:

Marian and the Elders
Accused of fornication, a woman hails her church into court.—*Time*, March 26, 1984

Church Guilty of Slander
Leona McNair filed a suit in 1979 after Roderick Meredith, an official of the Worldwide Church, used an annual ministers' meeting and a church magazine to publize the intimate details of her divorce from Raymond McNair, another church official and Meredith's brother-in-law.—*Pasadena* (Cal.) *Star-News* August 24, 1984

San Jose Parishioner Files Suit
Against Church, Counselor
A former member of a Fundamentalist church has filed a $5 million lawsuit claiming that marital and sexual problems confided to a marriage counselor were told to the entire congregation during a Sunday service.—*Los Angeles Herald*, April 10, 1984

Obviously, something is wrong today, either with the church, the individuals who are being disciplined, or the society that reacts to news of discipline in the church. Just what is discipline anyway, and how should it be practiced in a litigious society?

The Intent and Purpose of Church Discipline

In the history of the church, discipline and consolation have always been combined in pastoral care. In *A History of the*

Cure of Souls, John T. McNeill examined the relationship between the authority of a pastoral guide and the authority of the guided person. He found wide variations within Christianity. The sacrament of penance, a basic modern Roman Catholic confessional practice, assumed obedience by the parishioner to the priest. McNeill describes Protestantism as being in favor of less intimate supervision and inclined to have control over the conduct of individual members exercised by the church at large. Scotland was the most prominent example of public church discipline; this discipline began with a pastoral spirit in which solicitous concern was shown for a sinner to repent rather than to be subjected to censures and penalties. Soon censures and penalties were invoked against nonconformists, and the system drifted into legalistic and negative trivialities and thereby lost authority in society as well as in the church.[1]

McNeill called for a renewal of discipline as part of a religious counselor's spiritual expertness. This expertness was to rest upon an established tradition or ecclesiastical system, for the clergy person represented more than individual professional competence. The individual qualities of saintly humility, unusual spiritual wisdom, and personal insight should be combined with authority beyond the self in church, scriptures, and the power of God manifest in the Holy Spirit.[2] Characteristics of the modern spiritual director are surveyed by Tilden Edwards in *Spiritual Friend.*[3]

The history of the cure of souls shows that church discipline is most effective when discipline is balanced with consolation and when the skill and compassion of the individual spiritual director is combined with ecclesiastical authority.[4]

The Biblical Balance

The Balance of Discipline and Consolation in the New Testament

Judgment and acceptance are interrelated in the New Testament. This may be seen from a study of some of the Greek words that are associated with the care of people in the New Testament. The most frequently used Greek term is *parakaleō,* which has a variety of meanings that bring together discipline and consolation.

Parakaleō is used in the Synoptic Gospels to indicate a cry for help (Mark 1:40; 5:18; 7:32; 8:22). Jesus' response to the cry for help is acceptance and restoration of help.

Exhortation is another meaning of *parakaleō*. Sometimes exhortation appears as an appeal to others who need help. It is a demonstration of the call of Jesus for all to come to him when they are weary and heavy-laden. To issue this call is to act as an ambassador of God (Luke 3:18; 2 Cor. 5:20).[5]

When a person is willing to receive help, then *parakaleō* becomes encouragement. This is the theme of the letter to the Hebrews, which the author describes as a "word of exhortation" (Heb. 13:22). Judgment is combined with acceptance. Readers are exhorted to be like those who have faith and keep their souls and not to be like those who shrink back and are destroyed (Heb. 10:36–39).

A companion word to *parakaleō* is *oikodomeō,* which is often translated as "building up" (Eph. 4:12). This is edifying conversation and thought within "the sight of God" by which believers grow strong and resist quarreling, jealousy, anger, and other sins (2 Cor. 12:19–20).

A more judgmental term is *noutheteō,* "admonish." Although there is a touch of sternness or blame in several of the uses of this term (1 Cor. 4:14), the word is combined with acceptance in the usual translation, "mutual instruction" (Rom. 15:14; Col. 3:16). The word stands for the motivation and action of a shepherd who guards the sheep (Acts 20:31).[6]

The Purposes of Discipline in the New Testament

In the New Testament and in the history of the church, discipline has had at least three purposes.

The first of these is the reformation and reconciliation of sinners. The letter of James concludes advice to the church with these words: "My brethren, if any one among you wanders from the truth and some one brings him back, let him know that whoever brings back a sinner from the error of his way will save his soul from death and will cover a multitude of sins" (James 5:19–20). Since the first purpose of discipline is reformation and reconciliation, the apostle Paul explains in 2 Corinthians the motivation for his emphasis upon discipline in 1 Corinthians, "For I wrote you out of much affliction and anguish of heart and with many tears, not to cause you pain but to let you know the abundant love that I have for you" (2 Cor. 2:4).

One reason for this later explanation was a fear by Paul that the Corinthian church had been too severe in the punishment of an offending member. Now that some discipline had been acted upon, the apostle urges "you should rather turn to forgive and comfort him, or he may be overwhelmed by excessive sorrow. So I beg you to reaffirm your love for him" (2 Cor. 2:7–8).

In a study of discipline in the history of the church, Thomas C. Oden refers to admonition *(noutheteō)* as correction when things go wrong and confrontation when there is repeated wrong. But, he adds, "it is not a coercive act that would manipulate change, but a respectful dialogue that holds possibilities for the voluntary redirection of behavior."[7] The fathers of the church sought a corrective temper in love, mutuality, and trust rather than in harsh tones of blaming, despairing, or condemnation. The examples of Cyprian and Gregory of Nazianzus are cited by Oden. This sense of admonition in the context of love is in keeping with the urging of Paul to the Christian leaders at Thessalonica (1 Thess. 5:14).

The second purpose of discipline is health of the fellowship. Through the Holy Spirit the church is to be presented to Christ "without spot or wrinkle or any such thing," but "holy and without blemish" (Eph. 5:27). Specific New Testament references to discipline are within the context of a concern both for the redemption of the sinner and for the health of the church (Matt. 18:15–20; 1 Cor. 5:1–5; 1 Thess. 5:14; 2 Thess. 3:6–15; 1 Tim. 5:20; Titus 1:13; 3:10).

The fellowship is to be protected through vigilance concerning the health of both pastor and people. One of the distinguishing marks of the American tradition of "a gathered fellowship" has been an insistence upon evident marks of spiritual conversion in the attitudes of a pastor and evidence of the "fruit of the Spirit" in his or her life.[8] Through this insistence upon discipline for both pastor and people, the American churches maintained the second major balance in discipline, which was an appropriate concern both for the needs of an individual and the goals of a congregation. This was also in keeping with the ancient practice of the "desert fathers" of the early church, who required that every spiritual director was to be under the guidance of someone else.[9] The spiritual maturity of the pastor was a guarantee against two extremes. One of these was a sentimental acceptance of any conduct through "acceptance" without ethical criteria. The other extreme was harshness, usually motivated by unresolved and unconscious conflicts of a punitive pastor. The ideal pastor who combines discipline and consolation would be one with "a spirit of power and love and self-control" (2 Tim. 1:7).

What is required of the pastor would also be required of the people. Effective discipline, from a New Testament point of view, takes place not only in order that the health of the fellowship may be maintained but also because the fellowship is healthy enough to exercise discipline with a balanced spirit of love and self-control. There must be some spiritual health in the fellowship in order for healing to take place through the discipline of the one and the many.

The third purpose of discipline is guidance for the community. This purpose is closely related to the previous one. Unless the community is instructed concerning the meaning of righteousness and the practice of judgment and acceptance, we will not know the standards by which discipline is to be exercised or the way in which the discipline may be redemptive. The New Testament passages about discipline include this element of instruction, both for the church and the community that looks at the church (1 Thess. 5:14; 1 Tim. 5:20; Titus 1:13; 3:10).

The early settlements on the American frontier were in special need of discipline as guidance for the community at large. In his study of "Churches as Moral Courts of the Frontier," William W. Sweet gave many accounts of the moral disorganization of the "revolutionary years." He quoted the statement of a Dartmouth College graduate in 1799 that only one member of the class was publicly known as a professing Christian. The evidence for this lack of profession was seen on most social occasions. House raisings, log rollings, weddings, and funerals frequently degenerated into drunken brawls. Abraham Lincoln observed, as a clerk in New Salem, Illinois, that "everybody came on Saturdays to trade, gossip, wrestle, raffle, pitch horseshoes, run races, get drunk, maul one another with their fists, and indulge generally in frontier happiness, as a relief from the week's monotonous drudgery on the raw and difficult farms."[10] Early county court records contained many charges of rape, divorce, bigamy, and adultery.

Moral restraint on the poorly policed frontier was provided primarily by Baptist, Presbyterian, and Methodist churches. The record books of early Baptist churches west of the Alleghenies were a catalog of frontier disorder: accusations of adultery, betting, fraudulent business dealings, calling someone a liar, destroying corner trees, lying, fighting, dancing, gambling, immoral conduct, intoxication, hypocrisy, talebearing, misusing a wife, nonattendance at church, carnal plays, quarreling, running an incorrect boundary line, selling an unsound mare, stealing, swearing, or threatening a slave. In one instance, slaveholders were disciplined for not allowing a slave to see her child.

Discipline was not only taught through actions in the church but also through preaching to the public in camp meetings. Boldness of spirit was required by those who were willing to preach to audiences that often included rowdies, who would break up exhortations against their violent ways by making as much noise or playing as many tricks as possible on the preacher and some of his pious hearers. The energy of these rioters was often exceeded by that of the vigorous circuit riders, such as Peter Cartwright. On one occasion, the "captain of the rowdies" was "struck down" (seized with religious convulsions) among the penitents just as he was about to quietly hang a string of frogs around the preacher's neck. On another occasion Cartwright knocked a rowdy chief from his horse with a club and, having captured him, saw to it that he was fined a sum of fifty dollars.

The Four Pastoral Functions in the New Testament

When the three purposes of discipline are understood in the light of New Testament and historical examples, the balance of judgment and acceptance places discipline under the general function of "reconciliation" (2 Cor. 5:19ff.). Reconciliation combines the two modes of forgiveness and discipline in the history of the church.[11] Reconciling as a part of pastoral care is consistent with the other pastoral functions of healing, sustaining, and guiding.

As a pastoral function, reconciliation combines the experience of being judged with the feeling that you are accepted in spite of the judgment. A psychoanalyst, Hannah Colm, refers to this type of discipline as "healing as participation."[12] Dr. Colm agrees with Paul Tillich that a suffering person cannot feel accepted if the therapist is silent or neutral. Patients are helped when they encounter a person who knows them deeply enough to judge them as they are and still be accepting of them. The function of the therapist or pastor is to open contacts with the world for the patient through the therapist and by judgment acceptance, to assist the patient in the elimination of unconscious defenses. This process is considered to be like that of psychiatrist Harry Stack Sullivan's "Participant Interaction." It is a challenge to the earlier idea of Freud, continued by some modern therapists, that the therapist is a blank screen and that such hiddenness and ethical neutrality is therapeutic. In this pastoral sense, discipline is participation with the sinner rather than withdrawal from the sinner.

In modern society, the situation is reversed. Moderns assume that a person is rejected if there is any reference to discipline. But Joseph Sittler accuses modern society of using "acceptance" in a loose manner. He characterizes the modern understanding of acceptance as saying "nothing for sure can be known; nothing is more certain than other things; no way is better than other ways; no structure or vision, quest, discipline, or evaluation is higher than others. No person is closer than another to the reality of authentic manhood, for all live in pathos, deception, and pitiable pride."[13] With this definition, "acceptance" becomes a general term for superficial deception and avoidance, "the courtesy of nonsignificance." In contrast, New Testament terms for discipline and compassion are filled with personal involvement: listener, witness, ambassador. Those who are in personal dialogue through discipline are living out their story of God in a concrete situation involved with another human person for whom they care.

The Structure of Discipline

Since discipline is related to valued priorities, there will inevitably be discussion about the structure of discipline in the organization of a Christian community, the church. But the structure of discipline immediately becomes a problem when a definition of the church is sought. If the church as known in society is identified with the body of Christ as presented in the New Testament, then discipline is a formidable undertaking. Who has ever maintained a pure and incorrupted church upon earth? The book of Acts is filled with illustrations of the problem: maladministration of the dole, deceit, controversy over missionary aim and personnel.

In the early church, the Donatists insisted upon the purity of church members as a guarantee of devotion to the church as the spotless bride of Christ. All were excluded when their actions or attitudes fell short of perfect dedication to Donatist ideals.

In answer to this problem of church discipline, Augustine developed a two-church theory. One church was pure and invisible; this church included every person predestined by God for salvation. The other church was visible but not entirely pure; it included only living persons who professed to believe in Christianity, some who were indeed destined for salvation and some who were not.

With this view of two churches, Augustine sought to provide some balance in discipline. The church would strive for purity, by excluding obvious and gross sinners, but would recognize that not all sins are known and that even known sins must be dealt with in a redemptive manner. This was considered possible through formulas for repentance, especially acts of penance.

Unfortunately, social and ecclesiastical forces could not maintain the necessary balance between judgment and mercy. The medieval church developed as a geographic unit in which all persons were members by the mere fact of residence in a parish. Furthermore, discipline was narrowed into an anonymous confession of sins to a priest and the practice of ritual acts.

In revolt against this demographic membership and institutionalized discipline, Anabaptists, Puritans, and others developed the concept of a "gathered community" in which signs of saving faith guaranteed admission to church membership. By the nineteenth century, the demographic church and the "believers' church" could be distinguished sociologically as well as theologically. Ernst Troeltsch described the "church type" as a parish system of Christianity supported by political as well as ecclesiastical organizations. In contrast, the "sect type" rejected political and worldly power and concentrated on life in the body of Christ for those who openly professed salvation as adults and submitted to strict requirements for continuing membership.

These distinctions of Troeltsch were developed in Europe and were blurred by the rise of denominations, in the American colonies and, later, on the expanding frontier. Problems of discipline became acute when a band of believers, such as the Methodist societies, became prominent enough to receive the social respect that in Europe was accorded to the established church.

The question of visible church (known to humans) and invisible church (known only to God) was often connected with questions concerning church membership. The early American ideal was a "declaration of experiences of a work of grace."[14] Questions were asked by the congregation of candidates for membership. What were the "experiences" that led converts to believe they had been "awakened"? It was assumed that the experience was a sign of God's grace, but candidates would have only an imperfect assurance of salvation during this life. For this reason they would be humble in their affirmation and would depend upon the church for some assurance that they were among the elect (known to God).

With this ideal, the American churches sought to make judgments concerning the entrance into church fellowship, the continuing development of disciples, and the occasional dismissal or reconciliation of members. The churches usually did not assume that their membership was pure.

There were two reactions to this "lukewarm" Christianity: a "holiness" emphasis through the Niagara Bible Conferences and the dispensationalism of the Scofield Reference Bible. The Bible Conference emphasis was upon the purity of the believer in a "sect-type" fellowship. The emphasis of the Scofield Reference Bible was upon the impurity of all organized churches and the possibility of salvation only for a remnant who adhered to the "fundamentals" of the faith.[15]

In the twentieth century, the question of membership is salient for the resolution of questions about discipline. If persons are accepted as members of a congregation by virtue of birth or superficial assent to a creed, they may legally reject public discipline, since they gave no assent to this requirement for membership in the church. On the other hand, a "sect" group may not only have experiential requirements for membership but may also demand continuing commitment to ethical and ecclesiastical goals for "good standing." If it is understood from the beginning of membership that the discipline of a member may include public expulsion, the church is ethically and probably legally secure in the practice of discipline against anyone who complains or who brings litigation against the church.

Discipline was not only related to the structure of the church in membership but also in the life-giving association between members, which was called the covenant. The covenant, a dominant concept for the relationship of Israel to God and the church to Christ, was central to early American concepts of church structures.[16] The covenant was known through the presentation of doctrine and the teaching of moral standards. Those who accepted these doctrines and lived by this conduct were considered to be part of the covenant community. In addition to intellectual and behavioral guarantees, there was the inner testimony of saving faith. This testimony was made known to the congregation in the recounting of an experience of grace. When all these factors were combined, the person was considered to live an "orderly life" within a community of grace. A statement of the covenant was developed by various denominations and was often recited in union by members who gathered for participation in the sacrament of communion. Communion was, in fact, the visible sign of the covenant. On the American frontier, members of Presbyterian churches came together every three months for communion. This was preceded by several days of prayer, preaching, and the examination of members by elders. If a person was considered to be "walking orderly," he was given a token of admission to "the Lord's Table." The communion table was set in a clearing and enclosed by a wooden fence. Those who had tokens for communion would come to an opening in the fence and present them to an elder. This type of discipline was referred to as "fencing the table."[17]

As individualism became more dominant in American churches of the nineteenth century, the covenant was neglected, both in preparation for communion and as a source of disciplined fellowship between members.

Some sense of discipline was maintained into the twentieth century in the structure of church authority expected of pastors and the board of governance, which might be composed of elders, vestry, or stewards. The major emphasis of authority was discipleship, the acceptance of God's judgment upon the life of an individual. Discipleship was shown through repentance of sin and submission to divine commands. Those who held authority over others were to lead in a shared appraisal of the needs of others for one Lord. Any acceptance of their admonitions was by free consent of the individual members. The demand for some sense of mutual authority and commitment was based upon New Testament statements concerning mutual instruction, primarily from the Greek word *noutheteō* (Rom. 15:14; 1 Cor. 4:14; 10:11; Eph. 6:4; Col. 3:16; 2 Thess. 3:15).

The Practice of Church Discipline

In the early church, whenever there was a need for individual correction by the congregation, the congregation expressed this first through a concerned individual, then through a group of individuals, and finally through corporate action (1 Cor. 5).

The progression of power demonstrates the limitation of individual authority. One Christian may be a witness to another, but only a congregation of believers can act to discipline a member.

Although Peter directly condemned Ananias and Sapphira (Acts 5:1–4), and Paul warned against the sins of individuals (1 Cor. 5:5), the proceedings for discipline in the New Testament were clearly to be carried out by a group. No ordained or unordained member of the congregation pronounced judgment alone. As churches developed more structure, a variety of emphases could be seen in the practice of church discipline.

The initial emphasis of discipline was upon reformation of sinners through confession and public disclosure. But by the middle of the ninth century, Frankish councils began to insist upon secrecy in confession. In Irish church law, the divulgence of a confession was one of the four offenses so grave that no penance was possible. Confession and penance grew in the Middle Ages into exclusive practices by the clergy that were wholly disassociated from church assemblies.[18] Discipline became an authoritative action of the clergy, guided by the rules of penitential manuals.

Public church discipline was revived by John Calvin and strongly implemented in the Scottish church by John Knox. A form of public repentance was provided by Knox in the 1564 *Book of Common Order.*[19] This emphasis came to the colonial churches in America and was the common practice on the frontier in the early nineteenth century.

A second emphasis in church discipline was upon the health of the fellowship. This was also concern of the early church and was revived whenever there was also a revival of emphasis upon the reformation of sinners. The health of the fellowship was especially strong in the class meetings of the Methodists. To uphold the purity of the church and to keep weak people from straying, a class leader or "circuit rider" might regulate a man who whipped his wife or told stories about other people. The regulation might include exclusion from communion, and in time the person might be banned from the society. When the Methodists organized churches with settled pastors, decisions concerning exclusion from the church were made by the congregation.

The authority of the congregation over the life of individual members did not survive the upward change of social circumstances in the late nineteenth century among major denominations. In 1851, Professor W. J. Sasnett of Emory College,

Georgia, wrote that many of those "whose position in society secures to them a leading influence, are adverse to the humbling spiritual exercises appropriate to class meetings, and it is under the blighting spell of their indifference, if not actual opposition, that the Church in many quarters regard them with unconcern."[20]

Whatever the particular emphasis might be in church discipline, the practice was designed to offer both a reproof and a comfort at every stage of development. Therefore, beginning with ancient practice of Matthew 18:15–20, a person first received an opportunity of reconciliation in private conversation with a brother. If this was not enough, several witnesses met with the person for mutual admonition. Only after this process could any public discipline take place.

Problems in the Practice of Discipline

Although the practice of discipline was designed to move from confrontation to consolation, it was difficult to maintain a balance. In his study of discipline in the early church, K. E. Kirk noted the growth of formalism, rigorism, and legalism.[21]

Because of these tendencies, discipline often declined in various periods of church history, only to appear again with renewed strictness at a later time. Morgan observes that the Puritans in England went to the extreme of frequent excommunication of members for minor offenses, probably in reaction against the Anglican churches, which were lax in discipline.[22]

Not only were there problems concerning the balance of confrontation and comfort, the criteria of judgment also had to be considered. Frontier churches in America were primarily concerned with gross misconduct such as wife beating, adultery, cheating, gossip, and public drunkenness. But the list grew longer as the churches became more respectable and ended in a trickle of small restraints concerning social taboos such as dancing or the wearing of makeup.

Another problem in discipline was the rising respectability of the mainline denominations after the Civil War and the increased individualism of American society in the outburst of private capitalism. The fellowship of the church was no longer needed as much as it had been on the frontier, and the Christian emphasis upon submission and repentance made little sense in a robust, expanding society of "self-made" people. In his review of the demise of discipline in the United States, Thomas Oden refers to the "unrestrained individual freedom" of the twentieth century.[23]

Conclusions

Several conclusions may be drawn from the success and failure of church discipline in the past in order that a renewal of church discipline in the present may be effective.

First, the theory and practice of a "gathered community" is essential. Unless persons enter a Christian fellowship with commitment and through a clearly understood covenant, they are unlikely to respond favorably or with understanding to any attempts at discipline.

Second, a church that balances the needs of individuals with the comfort and admonition of a caring community will be in a better position to exercise discipline without harshness or resentment. The sharing of burdens and failures can be such a regular part of church life that correction and comfort from others will be expected. If this is the basic spirit of the congregation, the individualism and isolation of modern society will be diminished in the congregation. More will be gained by sharing and correction than by isolation and withdrawal.

A third emphasis would be on the speaking of truth in a spirit of love and self-control. If a congregation is accustomed to confrontation alongside forgiveness and acceptance, the secular practices of concealment and contempt will be given up. In contrast to this emphasis, the practice of concealment and defense of status in the modern church is so great that any disclosure of truth about a person is inconsistent with what people expect a modern and worldly church to be. It is no wonder that ligitation ensues from these unexpected and infrequent confrontations.

A fourth expectation would naturally follow from this: the necessity of constant inner discipline as a meaning of discipleship. If this is the practice of the individual disciple, encouragement and admonition in small groups will be welcomed. Each individual will feel the necessity of doing what is expected of others. And when all share in this expectation, all can assist one another in mutual discipline.

In contrast to mutual discipline are the clashes between those who have been disciplined and the pastor or church staff responsible for the discipline. Since there was no group cohesion to begin with, the discipline appeared as a power play by a professional person against a member who was dissatisfied with the judgment rendered. Discipline would not appear to be effective unless pastor and people practice discipline together and share mutually in all things, including speaking the truth in love and self-control.

It is also obvious from the history of church discipline that the practice has steadily deteriorated whenever cultural modes of behavior were mixed in with basic requirements of Christian character. This means that the church not only must maintain purity through the discipline of individuals who dissent from accepted practice, but that the church must determine what the accepted practice is to be in every generation. There must be renewed study of the scriptures to distinguish that which is "the fruit of the Spirit," marking a person as faithful in a Christian fellowship, from the practices that are deemed respectable by a race, region, or social class.

Finally, it is absolutely necessary for discipline to be seen as a part of pastoral care. Discipline and consolation, reformation and reconciliation, fellowship and guidance are all part of the practice of discipline. It is difficult to bring all these elements to bear upon the case of a problem individual, but it is also clear that we have a greater problem when any of these elements are missing.

If churches exercise discipline in such a balanced way, the chance of a malpractice suit will be greatly lessened. Perhaps the possibility of such suits will force the churches to reexamine their disciplinary procedures in the light of the Bible and of the experience of the church in past ages.

5

Helping When the Risks
Are Great

Thomas L. Needham

Following the malpractice suit against Grace Community Church, pastors began to make anxious inquiries about the future of their counseling ministries. Some responded with resignation, saying, "Well, I guess we've lost another domain to the professionals." Some expressed concern about their vulnerability with lay counseling ministries, asking, "Will it be safe to continue this type of ministry?" Some became more sensitive about deciding whether a parishioner was demon-possessed or mentally ill, asking, "What's the difference? What do you think about this particular case?"

Each of these questions points up anxiety over clergy and lay involvement in helping troubled individuals. Even though the church "won" when the Nally suit was dismissed by the courts, the case had a negative impact on insurance companies, and it also left an indelible concern in pastors' minds over their vulnerability for counseling in the local church—and rightfully so. The central question becomes: How can we maintain and expand our lay and pastoral counseling ministry while preventing or reducing our vulnerability to lawsuits? In this chapter, we will seek answers to this question by pondering three additional questions: What are potentially high-risk situations? Why are the risks increasing? and How can we care carefully?

What Are Potentially High-risk Situations?

Potentially high-risk situations can result from programs and actions of pastoral and lay counselors as well as from the general philosophical framework of the church. Each of these can lead to effective or noneffective helping strategies. While some of the risks discussed are direct violations of ethical or legal codes (i.e., lack of confidentiality, sex with a counselee), most have been included because: (1) they reflect poor judgment for counseling intervention; (2) they go beyond acceptable practices in mental health or pastoral counseling; and (3) they increase the risk of embarrassing, complicating, or harming the person seeking help.

The potential risks listed below can be single actions or a cluster of beliefs and actions:

1. Administration, interpretation, and storing of personality and psychological tests

2. Belief in simple spiritual solutions for complex emotional and psychological problems

3. Belief that all problems are spiritual or physical, with a denial of emotional and psychological dimensions

4. Belief that pastoral and lay counselors need only biblical training to solve such severe problems as neuroses, psychoses, and suicidal intentions

5. Belief that sincerity and good intentions are the major ingredients in pastoral and lay counseling

6. Belief that pastors should be all things to all people

7. Counseling psychotic and suicidal individuals

8. Counseling a mentally incompetent patient

9. Advising against medical or psychological treatment

10. Counseling regarding psychiatric medications

11. Denial of the existence or severity of a psychological or psychosomatic disorder

12. Improper care of records

13. Inadequately trained lay and pastoral counselors

14. Failure to give credence to violent intentions or statements

15. Misdiagnosing psychotics as demon-possessed

16. Misrepresenting one's title, position, degrees, or abilities (i.e., psychologist, psychotherapist)

17. Poorly supervised lay counselors

18. Recommending divorce

19. Sexual relations with a counselee

20. Violations of confidentiality (by ministerial or secretarial staff)

After examining this list, you may wonder how beliefs can be included in a list of potentially high-risk situations. They have been included because beliefs usually undergird actions. Since beliefs, like those listed in numbers two through six, have a direct influence on the type and extent of one's training, supervision, consultation, and use of referral sources, they are recognized as potentially problematic in their outcome. How can this be?

If a pastor and his or her constituents hold to items three or four above and have an active lay-counseling ministry, then the pastoral and lay counselors will find themselves giving simple suggestions to very complex personal problems. The characteristic referral, if one is made, will be to a physician rather than to a mental health professional. Such was the case when a psychotic young woman preoccupied with a scissors heard voices telling her to cut off her hair. After making immediate arrangements for a counselor to see her, she canceled her appointment, saying that her church lay counselor told her she didn't need to see a professional; rather, she should come to the church and they would pray for her. The fact that she was counseling weekly with this lay person and was not encouraged to see a psychiatrist or clinical psychologist, demonstrated poor judgment that was allowing her emotional health to deteriorate as well as endangering her life.

In another case, a young mother developed chronic insomnia during a period of time that she was being counseled by pastoral and lay leaders in her local church. But no one had adequately diagnosed her problem of depression as being due to her marital and family unhappiness. Before becoming a wife and mother, she had been career-oriented. But as a young mother, she was advised by church leaders that the mother's place was in the home and that she needed to bring her husband to the Lord. She would not be "truly happy until her 'unsaved' husband was converted." Since the church also took a strong stand against divorce, that option of resolving her marital problem was closed. She felt trapped. How could she expect to be happy? If those counseling with her had worked with her to identify the problem, some possible solutions would have been opened to her: breaking through the unrealistic expectations that as a mother she would spend most of her time with the baby; moving out of her isolation by developing friendships; examining her career needs and considering part-time employment until she was more comfortable in spending time away from the infant; and beginning to understand that communication with her husband, whether saved or not, would greatly enrich her marriage. A realistic identification of the problem is always essential to finding workable solutions.

Sometimes, pastoral or lay counselors misdiagnose severe psychotic states, such as calling a paranoid schizophrenia demon possession, thereby endangering the physical welfare of those who come in contact with the paranoid individual. One morning I received an urgent phone call from a local pastor seeking advice in just such a case. He had been called upon to say a prayer of exorcism in a house where a young man was struggling with voices that were telling him to kill his parents. It seemed as though the family was going from church to church, asking pastors to exorcise their home and son. They believed this was a difficult demon and that it would just be a matter of time before they got the right pastor to free their son from this evil force. My advice to the pastor was to help the family hospitalize this young man immediately, where his bizarre thoughts could be brought under control with medication. Then, after reducing the risk of suicide or homicide through medication and hospitalization, the spiritual-psychological treatment process could be initiated.

In these types of situations, I find that novices increase the risk of harm to someone, and reduce or eliminate the possibility of healing, by making three common errors: (1) diagnosing most if not all bizarre behavior as a form of spirit possession, (2) overemphasizing the instantaneous release of the individual without equivalent concern for a loving and sometimes lengthy helping relationship before and after the exorcism, and (3) overemphasizing the ability to exorcise, rather than the ability to follow the timely leadership of the Holy Spirit in leading the individual to deliverance.

Psychological testing poses another area of vulnerability for the pastoral or lay counselor. In the hands of a skilled interpreter, test results can provide invaluable timesaving insights into various dimensions of an individual's personality functioning. However, the interpretation of test results is a skill, a skill that develops with knowledge of human behavior, knowledge about the test, and knowledge about the particular person being tested. Without this skill, interpretation can be faulty at best, and, at worst, harmful. It can be harmful because people take psychological test information as "gospel truth." In marriage counseling, the information may be misused by one member of the couple who takes the other's problems as ammunition for further hostilities. Sometimes the evaluator may use the information as ammunition for a cause. On one occasion, a highly respected pastor persuaded an ordination committee not to ordain a young man, based on his Taylor Johnson Temperament Analysis test scores. The pastor contended that the test showed this individual to be unsuited to the ministry. Such conclusions, based on one test interpreted by a non-expert, would probably not stand the test of either a professional or legal challenge.

Other potentially high-risk situations, such as improper care of records, misrepresentation of one's title or abilities, and confidentiality, are discussed elsewhere in this book. Now let us consider why risks are on the rise for pastoral and lay counselors.

Why Are the Risks Increasing?

In a certain sense all growth in the number of contacts results in increased personal and legal risks. Some risks, however, are greater than others. Just how great the risks are that the church is taking when it reaches out to people's needs will only be known as suits are filed and decisions are handed down by the courts. This lack of judicial decrees should not deter us from taking a serious look at our vulnerability and at possible precautionary actions. In part, the procedures to help us avoid or diminish the possibility of lawsuits include understanding why and how risks are increasing and how we affect that situation by our own actions.

What are the reasons for the increasing risks of litigation? In this section we will discuss seven probable causes: (1) a litigious atmosphere, (2) increased demands for pastoral counseling, (3) new lay ministries, (4) a lag between intention and ability, (5) inadequate attitudes toward problems and problem solving, (6) inadequate training, and (7) inappropriate follow-up preaching after a suicide or other crisis situation.

A Litigious Atmosphere

This entire volume responds to the reality of the fact that, given an increasing emphasis on individual rights, people are increasingly turning to the courts to render damages when they feel wronged or harmed. As absurd as we may believe some of this litigation to be, it is nonetheless a reality that we must prepare to confront. There are also hostile attitudes toward the church, and people are looking for reasons to vent their frustration and anger against such overarching authority figures. The Grace Community Church suit startles us with this reality.

Increased Demands for Pastoral Counseling

In the past few years there has been a growing disillusionment among Evangelicals with the limitations of secular psychological solutions to problems of living. These same individuals are now looking to their church and their faith to find solutions that incorporate what they believe with their personal growth and problem solving. Martin Marty and others in their Gallup Poll study see this as a major trend of the eighties. They write:

> Adherents to religion will be increasingly aware of their own capabilities. They will not be so accepting of the past or easy answers to complex issues. They will be more sophisticated and will require a more stimulating educational and worship experience. They will need to see the relation between their beliefs and their self-development.[1]

In the Los Angeles area, these increasing demands are evidenced by the number of pastors and laity seeking graduate training and degrees in pastoral or marriage counseling, as well as the increasing number of churches that now have formalized counseling services. As these efforts mushroom, inadequate foundations and planning will expose churches to greater and greater risks.

New Lay Ministries

With increasing demands being placed on pastors for counseling, they are turning more and more to the laity for help. The proliferation of programs and training materials attests to this fact. However, at the Needham Institute in Los Angeles, we have encountered wide variations in the quality of these various efforts. We have found the highest standards to be among larger churches that can afford full-time mental health professionals to train and supervise their lay personnel in counseling. Less affluent churches tend to be more vulnerable because they are without knowledgeable professional input at the levels of training, supervision, and referral. However, without this input, counseling efforts, no matter how sincere, could open both the counselors and the church to lengthy litigation.

A Lag Between Intention and Ability

Peter intended to be loyal to Christ. While he was sincere, he lacked the ability to carry out his intention. Unfortunately, we are sometimes like Peter. Our hearts and heads are not together in our church outreach ministries. We confuse sincerity with spirituality and neglect the hard work of foresightful planning, training, and coordination. The church that makes a significant and low-risk effort to meet the challenge of the complex problems of its parishioners will be the church that carefully and adequately develops training materials, programs, supervision, and referral. The risks of complicating a person's problems are too great to enter into the realm of helping troubled individuals without the ability to back our intentions.

Inadequate Attitudes Toward Problems and Problem Solving

Closely related to the overzealous attitude are other attitudes equally inadequate. They relate to understanding the nature of deeper-seated problems and how to deal with them. What are these attitudes that increase our risks?

The risks are significantly increased by attitudes that contend that biblical and theological knowledge—that is, the knowledge of God—is all one needs when confronting the problems of living. Knowledge from the medical and psychological fields is seen as unimportant. Human knowledge is diminished or rejected rather than made to serve the purposes of God. Much of this avoidance results because some counselors have failed to maintain a commitment to the Christian faith. However, the efforts of Christian professionals and of institutions such as the Fuller Theological Seminary School of

Psychology have demonstrated that Christians can develop professional knowledge and skills related to clinical psychology and integrate that knowledge and those skills with a firm faith in Jesus Christ.

What if this dual training is neglected? Can churches take the risk of responding to sensitive and complex personal problems without training in both spiritual and psychological matters? No! Human behavior is very complex, and when churches offer aid to people, saying that they understand and can help people deal with complex problems, they take on moral, ethical, and legal responsibility. Whether one does this as a mental health professional, a pastoral counselor, or a lay counselor is irrelevant. Each must be able, at his or her own level of competence, to know and respect limitations and to recognize problems that need referral.

Inadequate Training

Whether for pastoral or lay counselors, incomplete training experiences leave one with blind spots, which in turn increase vulnerability without the counselor's even realizing it.

Proper training develops necessary attitudes, ideas, skills, and commitments and thus helps individuals to recognize their limitations. But these are not always easy to define, especially now with the growth of lay-counseling ministries.

Since lay counseling is of recent origin, at least in its widespread popularity, standards of training and conduct are not widely developed or followed. Therefore, churches must give very careful consideration to the selection, training, and supervision of lay counselors. Later in this chapter, we will discuss the training standards that we consider minimum.

Inappropriate Follow-up Preaching After a Suicide or Other Crisis Situation

Some ministers, in sincere eagerness to prevent further suicides or suicide attempts, may preach sermons about the sin of taking one's own life after they are startled by the death of such a parishioner. In view of the contemporary litigious atmosphere, the hostility stirred up through preaching that people who commit suicide go to hell is surely an unwise risk that seems likely to drive people to litigation.

How Can We Care Carefully?

In the light of the churches' movement toward counseling ministries, which brings with it higher risks of litigation, and in light of the churches' conscious and unconscious difficulty in relating realistically to the complex helping relationship, we are forced to ask if the church shouldn't abandon these laudable but risky efforts. While many pastors and churches will follow this trend of thought, I would like to suggest that the solution lies in taking precautions rather than in withdrawal. I believe the pertinent question is not "Should we continue to develop our counseling ministry?" but rather "How can we continue our caring efforts in the midst of a potentially difficult and unclear litigious atmosphere?"

Are there guidelines that can be followed to reduce the risk of caring ministries? How can we care without jeopardizing the local church with lawsuits? How can we expand and develop our caring ministries and reduce the risk of a malpractice suit? These are important questions. The answers I propose have evolved through the training and supervision of pastoral and lay-counseling ministries, as well as through discussions with experts in the disciplines of theology, psychology, sociology, ministry, and law. The answers that I have formulated for caring carefully are summarized by ten major guidelines.

Before we enumerate and discuss these guidelines, it is important to note that there are many other guidelines throughout this book, some related to insurance, some to defining the role of the pastoral counselor, some to legal issues and confidentiality. These guidelines will not be repeated in this chapter. We will focus here on training, supervision, assessment, levels of intervention, and the general care of troubled persons.

The ten guidelines are: (1) develop a formal counseling policy for your church, (2) develop adequate selection, training, and supervision, (3) avoid misleading claims, (4) make a thorough evaluation of the problem, (5) learn to benefit from testing, (6) determine your level of intervention, (7) make use of consultation and referral, (8) take advantage of continuing education, (9) guard records and information, and (10) provide follow-up care.

1. Develop a Formal Counseling Policy

The purpose of this policy is to establish the parameters and standards for the development and operation of a pastoral and lay-counseling program.

While chapter 2 deals with the legal significance of this statement, we will discuss the areas that need to be included in the general policy. The areas of discussion and policy-making should include:

Determining target needs

Assessing resources

Determining organizational channels and accountability

Establishing training and supervision standards

Establishing selection procedures

Determining the issue of fees or contributions

Formulating operational guidelines

Checking insurance coverage

Developing a feedback loop

As a church decides to expand its pastoral or lay-counseling ministries, there are specific considerations to be made in each of the above-listed areas. The reader should consult chapter 7 in this book regarding fees and insurance. The second guideline deals with selection and training. Let us begin here by asking, "What is the importance of defining needs?"

Determining target needs is essential for the training and supervision of lay counselors, in order to determine the kind of leadership and program needed to meet these needs. If the target needs include pastoral care and counseling to the bereaved, to those in marital conflict, to those with parent-child problems, to the depressed, and to the emotionally and physically ill, the training program will have to be extensive.

Assessment of human resources may lead to an interchurch effort. One pastor concluded, "I have the needs in my church for an extensive lay-counseling program, but I have few members who have the level of maturity needed to help others." The solution at this point can often be a cooperative effort involving several congregations.

While each local church is in some way responsible for the supervision of its leadership, the undefined and freestyle organizational structure of some independent churches make accountability for appropriate training and supervision difficult. In contrast, traditional denominational churches, more formally organized and supervised, will have less difficulty in maintaining uniformity of training standards and quality supervision. Whatever the organizational structure of one's church, the pastor should assume direct responsibility to ensure adequate organization, leadership, accountability, training, and supervision. This will include making provisions for guidelines for day-to-day operations.

Operational guidelines will include decisions about where counseling sessions will be held, how they will be scheduled and by whom, what lay counselors will handle which problems, whether or not the individuals will initially see a pastoral counselor or mental health professional, and how many sessions the lay counselor will provide per individual or family. These guidelines should lead to a maximum degree of courteous, confidential, and competent care. Only the most gifted lay counselors should extend themselves beyond six one-hour consultations.

Advertising one's counseling services is an integral part of establishing new programs and maintaining and expanding existing ones. However, advertising has serious drawbacks if it is not done knowledgeably and circumspectly. Churches should consider several important do's and don'ts.

Do state that your church cares about helping people in crisis. Do specify the educational and pastoral care services that are available to troubled individuals, couples, and families. Do state the counselors' qualifications, licenses, and limitations. Also, do consult with your church insurer about the insurability of advertising certain counseling claims. *But* do not use the legally protected words of licensed professionals (i.e., psychotherapy, psychological treatment/testing). Do not make claims for healing considered unethical if made by mental health counselors. Do not advertise counseling to the community at large without considering potential increases in risk and liability (see chapter 1 for litigation contending increased liability of a Jewish temple in Los Angeles based on advertising). And do not advertise pastoral ministries that go beyond biblical and theological guidelines (see chapter 2) without appropriate rationale and training.

"How will we decide we have provided a quality low-risk

ministry?" An evaluation process called a feedback loop will help to provide answers. Feedback loop is an organizational term that recognizes the dynamic, changing nature of organizations and that also recognizes that the most effective means of careful and productive expansion comes through input from users and providers of a given service. They can answer such questions as: "How effective are we in reaching the people and the problems we targeted? How helpful have we been to the people we serve? How efficiently have we offered our services? What areas of our program, training, supervision, and evaluation need changing?" Initially, these important issues need to be addressed regularly. After several years of successful operation, the evaluation process can be adequately conducted on an annual basis.

2. Develop Adequate Selection, Training, and Supervision

The individuals selected, the training program developed, and the supervision provided are in part determined by the goals set forth in the formal counseling policy. What are adequate programs in these areas? How do you ensure competence? Let us begin with the selection of lay counselors.

I recommend four criteria for selecting lay counselors. First, they should possess the same level of maturity required of all leaders in the church. Second, they should be able to respond empathetically, rather than judgmentally or critically, to people in trouble. Compassion is an essential ingredient in the caregiver. Third, they should show evidence of emotional maturity, flexibility, openness to feelings, and general adaptability, as evidenced on a reliable psychological test such as the Sixteen Personality Factors test. (Training in use of this test is available for ministers by contacting the Institute for Personality and Ability Testing, Champaign, Illinois.) Finally, they should be individuals who understand the time and energy commitment required in counseling two or three individuals or families per week. They should also be aware of the additional time needed for supervision and referral. Isolation will quickly lead to fatigue and burnout.

After the lay candidates are selected, they should be trained in a broad understanding of emotional and spiritual problems, in specific techniques for handling individuals in crisis situations, and in effective coping skills for their own lives.

At the Needham Institute, we provide this kind of training in thirty weeks (three hours a night once a week). This Basic Pastoral Counseling Program for ministers and laity addresses many key areas:

Spiritual, theological power for personality change

Developmental versus deep-seated psychological problems

Appropriate use of scripture and prayer in counseling

Listening skills and counseling techniques

Legal responsibilities

Religious disguises of hostility, depression, and denial

Special problems in crisis counseling

Referral procedures

Personality health of the counselor

Our program has been designed with theological, psychological, and educational integrity by experts in each field. The course begins with a strong theoretical foundation of understanding human development in its spiritual and psychological components and leads to practice in counseling and skill development, integrated with personal growth experiences. This carefully designed program results in highly skilled and motivated pastoral and lay care-givers. Many return to traditional positions in teaching, committee leadership, youth work, and family ministry, while some begin various counseling ministries relating to marriage and family problems, homosexuality, personal and social adjustment, depression, and reactions to grief.

For those in the latter categories, we recommend advanced supervision. This should follow the basic training. Small groups of eight to ten people provide continuing education through case discussions, consideration of theoretical issues, directed reading, workshops, and personal growth experiences. Under the leadership of certified pastoral counselors or licensed Christian mental health professionals, these pastoral and lay counselors receive this experience while they are counseling in their local church.

Having been carefully selected, trained, and supervised, the pastoral or lay counselor will enjoy a fruitful and careful ministry.

3. Avoid Misleading Claims

"You know most problems originate in the head. Doctors say as much as eighty-five percent of all physical problems are psychosomatic. If you get your life right with God, then you don't need a psychologist or a medical doctor." Such half-truths can do more harm than good. They can be misleading to people who are looking for spiritual solutions or who do not understand the complexity of human behavior.

Misleading claims are any personal or institutional claims that lead individuals to believe something that is not true—about one's degrees, training, license, titles, or skills or about treatment outcome. How can these be avoided?

The best prevention is a good training program. At the Institute, I have seen individuals who, as they began to see the difficulty of the counseling task, reduce their current claims and expectations in helping people. However, putting our claims in line with our abilities is not always easy. Let us consider two reasons.

First, within the Christian community, there is a tendency to generalize instantaneous transformations in all areas of human problems. Some claim that an omnipotent God must be able to cure all problems instantly. This kind of magical claim, whether presented to individuals or to the community at large, will certainly lead to the program's being discredited. It is also possible that a disgruntled individual may use this kind of claim as a basis for litigation against the church that made it.

Second, within the Christian community, I have frequently heard pastors misuse titles, saying, "Mr. A, a member of our church, is a psychologist or psychiatrist." At other times, I have heard pastors say, "Our lay counselors are as good as any psychologist." Certain titles and words are reserved for individuals with professional licenses. Misleading claims about the services one offers can also be a violation of the law.

4. Make a Thorough Evaluation of the Problem

As part of their training, pastoral and lay counselors should be taught to be thorough in evaluation of an individual's problems and resources. To assure this, I recommend five steps to take in the first interview:

1. Take a history

2. Use tests if you can

3. Determine chronicity and severity

4. Determine if psychotic, suicidal, psychosomatic

5. Evaluate the person's resources

Step One: Take a History. As one begins to develop background information on an individual, a helpful picture emerges as to how this individual solves problems. This information becomes the basis for deciding whether to counsel or refer the person. What kind of information is part of this history-taking process?

While the nature of some of the information varies by age and cultural background, there are consistent concerns. They include general physical health, emotional history and health, nutrition and diet (particularly important with underprivileged and elderly), current medications, history of previous counseling, marital and family history, present and past jobs, major stressors, and current relationships with other people.

How is this information obtained? An intake form can be completed by the individual before the first session, or else structured questions can be used during the first session. In either case, the information must be kept confidential.

Step Two: Use Tests. When possible, testing information should be part of the evaluation. Two commonly used instruments that provide the helpful and easily understood information are the Minnesota Multiphasic Personality Inventory (MMPI) and the Sixteen Personality Factors Test (16PF). While these tests also provide information regarding complex psychological states that require interpretation by a sophisticated clinician, there are relatively easy measures on both tests to assess the severity of an individual's problems and help determine whether the person is neurotic or psychotic.

Step Three: Determine Chronicity and Severity. Chronicity and severity are two important evaluative concepts. Chronicity deals with the length of time the problem has existed, and severity deals with impaired daily functioning. In order to determine how chronic and severe an individual's problem may be, the counselor needs to find answers to many pertinent questions: "Have there been any changes in eating habits? How about sleep habits: any difficulty in going to sleep? Does the person wake early, unable to return to sleep? Is the person withdrawing from relationships and becoming isolated? Are there other signs of increased anxiety and irritability? How long have these symptoms, tensions, and complaints existed? How much are these problems interfering with daily routines and functioning?"

The more chronic and consistent the changes in behavior patterns, and the more reduction of normal functioning, the more need there will be for professional intervention.

Step Four: Determine Whether Psychotic, Suicidal, or Psychosomatic. The pastoral or lay-counselor training program should provide information and training in distinguishing chronic problem patients, psychotics, and potentially suicidal individuals. As a general rule, pastoral and lay counselors should refer all individuals who have delusions (persecutory or grandiose) or hallucinations (visual, auditory, or tactile) or who are disoriented and unable to know who they are, where they are, or what day or month it is.

The pastoral or lay counselor should also recognize individuals who are at high risk to become suicidal. It is a myth that people who threaten suicide do not follow through with it. Every threat or mention of suicide should be taken seriously and evaluated. Progressive levels of seriousness are: (1) ideas about suicide, (2) plans to carry out the idea, (3) steps taken in securing the means—pills, gun, or other instrument. Increased vulnerability at any of the three levels occurs when the individual is psychotic, hostile, isolated, or seriously depressed.

Step Five: Evaluate the Person's Resources. Evaluation is not complete without an assessment evaluation of the individual's resources for solving his or her problems. "Is the person emotionally stable? Are there friends who will be supportive? What resources of faith and community does the person have? Does he or she have a physician? Are there financial resources or insurance if professional treatment is needed? What community resources might we need for backup?"

The answers to these questions are important because supportive caring relationships are an essential part of healing and growing. The more complex the problem, the more involved the supporting process becomes. If the person is dependent and uses passivity to manipulate others into problem solving, it will take a highly skilled counselor to break through the resistance to using one's own resources. The dependent person and the individual with limited personal resources will need professional care.

5. Learn to Benefit from Testing

We have already stated that tests such as the MMPI and the 16PF (see Step Two) provide valuable information regarding the assessment of psychotic and neurotic conditions. When used in an ethical and informed manner, test results can help to identify those people and problems that require consultation or referral, as well as to identify problems in persons not referred. How can we benefit from using tests ethically and in an informed manner?

The moral use of tests requires a knowledge both of the limitations of testing in general and of the uses and limitations of the selected test. One needs also to recognize one's limitations in understanding and interpreting a test. Some experts spend an entire lifetime developing expertise in diagnosing problems on the basis of a particular test. While there is room for less-informed test users, ministers and laity need to recognize their limitations and use tests with consultation and supervision close at hand.

Tests must be interpreted; therefore, the more we can learn about a given test, the more we can use it appropriately. Essentially, the areas to become informed about include how to use the information, what to tell the individual, how to store the information, and whether to view the scores as dynamic or static. The counselor needs to learn a healthy respect for the durability of personality, as well as to recognize the possibilities for change. There is a delicate balance between the permanency and the flexibility of personality, and the counselor's attitude will influence the individual's efforts and progress.

6. Determine Your Level of Intervention

What can be done to help a troubled person depends largely on the nature of the person's problem and the ability of the counselor. This requires an understanding of the levels of intervention, with the implications of each intervention. What are those levels?

The first level is the "standby" position, in which, after one or two interviews, the counselor encourages the person that the outcome will be favorable and then decides to wait and see how the individual will work out the problem. The door is left open for the person to return at any time, but he or she is not encouraged to remain for short- or long-term intervention. This option should not be used for suicidal or psychotic individuals, or in complicated situations. In these latter cases, consultation should be sought, usually without delay.

Sometimes the standby position may be needed to develop confidence in the relationship so that a referral can be made. Even seriously disturbed persons may not always be open to professional care. While the pastoral or lay counselor does not want to counsel this individual, it may not be possible to make an immediate referral. During this time, the counselor may comment occasionally at church or make a phone call, to build a sense of trust that can later be used for making the referral.

At the second level, the counselor is taking a more supportive role. If the counselor is a skilled listener, the troubled person is helped to think through issues and possible solutions. Empathetic listening also helps the person ventilate pent-up emotions. Encouragement and comfort are important. Generally, there is very little risk at this level.

Level three interventions include interventions that involve persons other than the counselee. Sometimes this is required by law; at other times it is in the best interest of the distressed person. In the former situation many state statutes require that counselors notify individuals who are likely to be the object of a counselee's violent urges. Most states also require ministers and counselors to report counselees who abuse children. Whether contacting the authorities or family members, one should first consult a psychiatrist or psychologist, as well as an attorney, because errors in violating confidentiality constitute malpractice in themselves.

Level four, uncovering repressed emotion, carries the highest risk. The counselor should not use uncovering techniques without understanding what he or she is doing and without being able and prepared to help the person develop an understanding of the significance of the charged emotional responses. While an individual may describe a traumatic experience without showing appropriately corresponding emotions, the *skilled* counselor can bring out these feelings. There are situations where the release of a repressed emotion is advisable as an important solution to a problem.

Since defenses operate for good reasons, we need to be sensitive, wise, and realistic about defensive resistances to feeling. Sometimes defenses seem to be literally impenetrable; at other times they are the frail shell that protects an inadequate personality from a frightening world. At still other times, they result from willful avoidance of change. Whatever the uses or reasons for defenses, counseling to remove them requires much skill and time.

7. Make Use of Consultation and Referral

More and more, mental health specialists have followed the lead of the medical profession in developing a team approach for evaluating and treating troubled persons. The pastoral or lay counselor should consistently and readily seek advice regarding any phase of the counseling process. In fact, an openness to this kind of continual growth process says something very positive about the counselor.

Since consultation involves divulging information and possibly referral, it is good to advise the individual of this from the beginning. You can say, "We frequently consult or refer to Dr. B. Since we are not experts in counseling, it may be necessary to seek advice on the most effective ways to help you."

Although making a referral will be frequently necessary, there are several reasons why it may be difficult. Most troublesome may be the frightened individual who is confronted in the referral by the severity of his or her problem. Such a person may make flattering and manipulative statements to the counselor to avoid referral, such as: "I am feeling so much better since I've been talking to you, do I really have to see Dr. B?" At other times he or she may ask: "Do you really think I am that bad?"

There are times when difficulty in referral is the result of an internal conflict within the counselor, who may have become attached to the counselee and thus encounters a problem in separating. Or a counselor may feel very inadequate over having to acknowledge limitations in helping skills.

However, neither the counselee's reluctance to be referred nor the counselor's reluctance to refer should block the referral process. Continuing a counseling relationship because one can not surmount this impasse is definitely a risky error of judgment.

On the other hand, using consultation frequently and developing referral sources and skills are both excellent ways to reduce the possibility of risk and error, while increasing the overall effectiveness of one's counseling technique.

8. Take Advantage of Continuing Education

Continuing education can take many forms and have many advantages. Chief among these is the increased ability to understand, evaluate, and counsel certain people and specific types of problems. Most health-care licensing and professional agencies require continuing education to ensure that the professional stays fresh in his or her approach and skills. While pastoral and lay counselors do not have this kind of ethical or legal demand for continuing education, there is the pressure of needing to minister effectively and in a careful manner.

In what area should the pastoral and lay counselor receive continued training? To a large extent, the answer to that question depends on previous experiences. Important areas of study are personality theory, abnormal psychology, developmental psychology, the integration of psychology and theology, group and individual counseling theory and methods, personal growth experiences for one's self, and training in special problems.

9. Guard Records and Information

Chapter 6 will deal with the importance of confidentiality in terms of the counselor divulging information, but let us discuss a few additional problem areas in confidentiality.

These concerns include indiscriminate accessibility to counseling notes and appointment calendars and improper storage of testing information. These can result in information getting into the wrong hands or being made public, with embarrassment to the parties involved. It does little good to stress confidentiality for lay counselors without taking additional steps to ensure total confidentiality.

The secretary who sets up the appointments must understand the legal, ethical, and psychological significance of keeping confidences. Both counselors and clerical-secretarial personnel must realize the importance of confidentiality to the helping relationship and agree to guard names, phone conversations, and in-house talks. Records should be kept in a locked filing cabinet, with restricted access to the key. As much as possible, adequate soundproofing or separation from other offices is needed to ensure that conversations will not be over-heard.

10. Provide Follow-up Care

Follow-up care should be considered an important part of a sensitive and careful caring ministry. Whether a person comes for help once or many times, pastoral and lay counselors are in a unique position for follow-up. Many isolated parishioners are cut off from the corporate resources of their church because they are shy, guilt-ridden, insecure, depressed, or confused about why Christians suffer. With attention to these problems, follow-up not only can reduce risks but can greatly enrich a church's counseling ministry.

First, the church counselor should be aware that important emotional and spiritual follow-up support can be provided for troubled individuals, couples, and families. Since bringing individuals to the point of being ready to tackle their problems is in itself an important accomplishment, counselors should view planting the seeds of caring and hope as essential. A troubled person may come once but become overly fearful about continuing, because verbalizing one's problems can be experienced as a frightening admission of failure. Another person may become frustrated with a believed inability to change and discontinue counseling for that reason. Still another individual will satisfactorily resolve the initial problem but remain detached from the church. In each of these situations, a friendly and caring phone call or handwritten note can provide the necessary encouragement for problem solving or involvement.

Second, follow-up is important because it provides information on the effectiveness of services rendered and may also point out an individual's fears and abilities in problem solving.

In this process of clarification, an important third result may occur: a bridge may be built between the individual and the local church. As the pastoral or lay counselor explores the disillusionments and misunderstandings of individuals, several common alienating beliefs are often uncovered. One such belief leads people to feel guilty when they suffer, in the conviction that all personal problems result from one's sin. While these kinds of deeply embedded belief systems often take extended time and support to change, the church counselor can reassure these individuals that their church actually seeks to free them from such ill-conceived teachings.

Finally, follow-up is important in eliminating resistances to referral. If the counselor has determined that a medical, legal, or mental health referral is important, it is appropriate to discuss with individuals their resistance to making the appropriate appointment. As discussed earlier in this chapter, in cases of suicidal or homicidal risk, pastoral and lay counselors may have a legal responsibility to follow up by involving others: family members, mental health professionals, or the local authorities.

Summary

The Nally lawsuit against Grace Community Church has left an indelible concern over the future of pastoral and lay counseling in the local church. I believe we should expand rather than reduce our helping efforts, and this requires that we understand why the risks are increasing. Following the ten suggested guidelines should help churches have an active, effective, and careful, caring ministry.

6

Confidentiality in the Pastoral Role

H. Newton Malony

When one tells something to a friend, it is normally expected that the friend will keep the secret and tell no one else. This is a matter of trust which, among good friends, is assumed and doesn't even have to be requested. Confidentiality between pastor and parishioner is based on this same kind of agreement. The parishioner assumes that the pastor will not gossip about what has been said and will not reveal it without permission. The parishioner's remarks have been shared in the confidence that the pastor can be trusted to keep them a secret.

Some pastors approach the matter quite differently, however. One pastor always begins his talks with church members this way: "Do you expect me to keep what you tell me in confidence?" "Yes, of course!" they reply. "Well, I have no intention of doing so," he answers. "I am simply the pastor of this church. It is the people of the church who minister. If I think of anyone who can help you, I intend to tell them about your problem and ask them to get in touch with you."

This is quite a different understanding of confidentiality from that of a pastor who says, "I always tell persons who come to me that I will not reveal anything they say to me to anyone— not even my spouse. What they say to me is similar to a confession made to a Catholic priest. I promise to act as if they can trust me to keep their secrets no matter what. They trust me to minister to them, and I will not violate that trust."

These pastors illustrate an important aspect of confidentiality, although they vary widely in their interpretation of how it should be expressed. They both are committed to the person's best interest, in spite of the fact that one concludes this can best be served by involving others while the second feels that no one should be told anything. Their differences are probably based on their understanding of the ordained ministry and the nature of the church, yet they are similar in their concern to act responsibly, as we shall see.

What Is Confidentiality?

Confidentiality refers to the act of protecting from disclosure that which one has been told under the assumption that it will not be revealed without permission. Although we are discussing pastors, other professionals, such as attorneys, physicians, and psychologists, also have relationships with persons in which confidentiality is an issue. We will compare these professionals with pastors later in this chapter. At this juncture it is enough to say that pastors are not the only ones concerned about confidentiality.

To repeat, in all cases, confidentiality presupposes a relationship in which a person confides information about him/herself under the assumption, stated or unstated, that it will be kept secret. For example, if we are diagnosed as having high blood pressure, we assume that the doctor will not tell anybody about it. Further, if we seek an attorney's advice on whether to sue a merchant who has cheated us, we assume that the attorney will not share this with anyone. And if we receive counseling from a psychologist about a compulsion to look under our bed before we go to sleep, we assume that the counselor will not communicate that problem to others. So it is with a pastor. If we seek pastoral help for a marriage problem, we assume that no one else—in the church or outside it—will be told about it.

This assumption concerning the relationship is an important first aspect of confidentiality. If this assumption is not present, there is no confidentiality required although certainly discretion should be exercised. Sometimes it is said that if a third person is present, confidentiality is not assumed. This may or may not be true—as in marriage counseling, for example—yet the point is still well taken that where a person *assumes* he or she is sharing information in confidence, confidentiality is involved.

The second major aspect of confidentiality is that of permission. Even if confidentiality is assumed in the relationship, the information may be shared with others if the person gives permission to do so. The pastor who said he might share with other church members what was being told to him illustrates the way in which permission is often obtained. A person who continued to talk after hearing the pastor say what he did would be giving permission for the information to be shared. A more typical situation might be one in which a person would ask a physician to tell another doctor about a specific physical condition in order to obtain a specialist's opinion. Sometimes pastors or counselors are asked by persons to state that they are good parents in child custody cases, for example. In these situations, the individual requests that information which was shared in confidence be shared. Under these conditions, within the scope of the permission granted, confidentiality does not apply.

There are several ways of looking at the giving of permission, however. A pastor may feel caught between a mother and a father when asked to testify in court on behalf of one of them. The pastor may have counseled both parents during a crisis in their marriage and might feel that each has strengths and weaknesses. In order to avoid this difficulty, some pastors tell couples when they first start talking with them that they will not become involved in any legal procedures in which they might have to reveal information that was shared in private, nor will they take sides in favor of either party.

On the other hand, it has been said that the right to reveal information lies with the person, not the pastor. Thus, if the person gives permission, the professional (pastor, physician, or psychologist) has no alternative but to testify. This is the case when one is served with a subpoena or a release-of-information form signed by a client or parishioner.

However, in the late 1970s a San Francisco psychiatrist refused to honor such a release. In spite of the fact that a former client had given permission for him to reveal certain information that had originally been shared in confidence—indeed, even requested that he do so—he refused. The judge in the case sentenced him to jail for three days. The psychiatrist appealed the judgment all the way to the United States Supreme Court but lost. He contended that he had a right to refuse to testify; he did not. Although he suggested that the trust other clients had in his promise that their conversations were confidential would be jeopardized, the judge contended that he could not withhold information when the person involved wanted it revealed.

A classic illustration can be seen in Victor Hugo's *Les Miserables,* in which the hero, Jean Valjean, confesses his identity as an escaped prisoner to a priest, who keeps his secret even though an innocent man is about to be convicted through mistaken identity. Jean Valjean himself confesses his identity to a stunned courtroom while the priest remains silent.

This leads us to a discussion of the uniqueness of the priest-penitent relationship, on which the right of pastors to remain silent about confidential information has been based.

Priest-Penitent, Pastor-Parishioner

Today's relationship between pastors and their parishioners stems from a relationship between priests and penitents that has developed over the last two thousand years of Christian history. Although these relationships are presently safeguarded under the rubric of "privileged communications," in which privacy is safeguarded by confidentiality, it was not always so.

In the early church, gossip was condemned and equated with such sins as slander (2 Cor. 12:20), maliciousness (Rom. 1:29), and idleness (1 Tim. 5:13). It was assumed that leaders would be free of these characteristics. However, the present tradition comes more likely from the authority Christ gave to the apostles to forgive or not forgive sins (John 20:23) and to permit or prohibit certain behavior (Matt. 16:19, bind or loose).

This authority appeared early in the history of the church in the act of the confession of sins. Penance was the act whereby judgment was pronounced, forgiveness offered, and retribution or recompense prescribed. In spite of the fact that there was much dialogue over whether the church was competent to forgive sins, by the fourth century the practice of confession and penance was fairly standard. Yet, interestingly enough, in most if not all cases the act was public rather than private.

In the Eastern Church the penitent went through four stages that began with prostrating himself or herself on the steps of the church and seeking the prayers of the people as they came to service. The process then included kneeling before the congregation and having special prayers said. It ended by restoration to the eucharist. In the Western Church, confession took place during Lent and included clothing the penitent with goat's hair and sprinkling the head with ashes. Holy Thursday was the time when public reconciliation occurred and the penitent was allowed to take Holy Communion.

These public acts gave way to private confession, however. The practice is thought to have begun in the British Isles and was standard throughout the church by the ninth century. Private confession became the norm. The act of penance became a sacrament, and confession of serious sins became a mandate. Church law required the priest never to reveal what had been told to him in this relationship.

What is known today as "clergy privilege" has become the rule by which most pastor-parishioner relationships are now understood. Although originally confined to what was told the priest in confession, many have assumed that it applies to whatever is told the pastor, be it in visiting the sick, administering the church, or counseling in the church office. All information gained by whatever means is assumed to be confidential, and the pastor is assumed to have an obligation, as well as a privilege, to remain silent about it.

It is helpful to realize that this pastoral privilege of not having to reveal what one knows is different from that accorded to the attorney. While both are based on the assumption that for society to be preserved certain relationships need to be safeguarded, clergy privilege is grounded in the relationship of persons to God, while attorney privilege is grounded in the relationship of persons to their accusers. By this is meant that western society has considered that reconciliation of the individual with God is of equal importance with the fair and unbiased administration of justice. Although one was based on church law and the other on common law, the intent is the same: namely, to assure that society continues to function in a cohesive manner.

The minister is considered to be an agent of God, just as the attorney is considered to be an agent of justice. Nothing is gained in the God-human relationship by public revelation of what was told the minister, and nothing is gained in the administration of justice by self-incrimination or by information forced from one's confidant. All persons have a right to ministry just as they have a right to counsel.

In addition to ministers and attorneys, spouses, physicians, journalists, and accountants are all protected from having to testify about what has been shared with them in confidence, on the basis that society considers these relationships especially important to maintain.

The Limits of Clergy Privilege

The obligation and the privilege of keeping confidential what one knows about another is not absolute. There are limits.

The legal opinion of Wigmore (1961) regarding the rules of evidence have generally been accepted as the conditions under which confidentiality functions. In addition to the conditions that the communication must have originated in the confidence that the information would not be disclosed, that confidence is essential for the satisfactory maintenance of the relationship, and that the relationship is one which society wants to foster, the decision rules that the injury to the relationship must be greater than the benefit to justice. This last condition requires a judgment both on the part of the professional, such as a pastor, and on the part of the judge who might require such a breach of confidence. Weighing the benefit to justice over against the relationship is not an easy task.

An example from the field of counseling illustrates the difficulty in this regard. A counselor was talking for some time with a man who confided that he had been abusing his child. The counselor believed that the man had been making much progress. In fact, he shared the information about child abuse while telling the counselor that he was not doing it as much as he had earlier. The counselor knew that the man had not revealed this to anyone outside his family and that, if apprehended, he would know immediately who had reported the matter to the police. The counselor thought, Will he stay in counseling if he finds out that I told the police? He probably would not. The counselor would have the problem of deciding whether the disruption of the relationship would be of less benefit than would be gained by seeing that justice was done and that the child was protected from abuse. (Some state laws now require professionals to report child abuse.)

This introduces a rule of thumb that has come to be used by professionals in these matters: namely, that confidence will not be breached unless the person is a danger to self or to others. In this case, the counselor might decide that the child was in real danger and would thus report the matter. However, the counselor could conceivably decide that the man was improving and that the child was not in immediate danger. In order to preserve the counseling relationship in which the man was obtaining help and to keep the family intact, the counselor would decide not to report the matter. Clearly, the question is complex, and the decision of whether to withhold or share information is one that can only be made after much thought.

Perhaps the best known example of this dilemma is that of *Tarasoff v. Board of Regents of the University of California.*[1] An outpatient at the hospital on the Berkeley campus informed his psychotherapist that he was planning to kill a young woman student when she returned to school in the fall. The therapist notified the campus police through a formal written request for assistance in dealing with a man he considered potentially dangerous to others. The campus police took the man into custody but released him when they found him to be rational. Hearing about the matter, the psychologist's supervisor requested that the letter to the campus police be returned and that it, along with the therapy notes from the session in which the man threatened the life of the young woman, be destroyed. Neither the intended victim nor her parents were warned.

Tatiana Tarasoff was killed by Prosenjit Poddar on October 27, 1969, and her parents filed suit against the University of California. Finally, after several court decisions, the case was settled out of court and resulted in a substantial amount of money being paid to the young woman's family.

Clearly, the issue was not a matter of whether the therapist warned the authorities or whether he misjudged the violent potential of the client. What was at issue was the failure to warn the intended victim. It is noteworthy that the professional has a duty to protect society from that which would disrupt it. Murder is clearly such a disruption.

Of related interest is whether a professional can predict violence with certainty. Some years ago a young man positioned himself in a tower on the University of Texas campus and sprayed the courtyard below with bullets that killed several police. It was revealed that he had talked of killing before that time in conversations with his psychiatrist. Many people felt that the psychiatrist should have assumed greater responsibility in reporting the matter, but the psychiatrist concluded that he was working with the young man on his violent impulses and that to report him before he did anything would have provoked him to leave therapy. Although his decision turned out to be in error, it is important to note that the California State Psychological Association[2] argued in the Tarasoff case that warning the possible victim would have been a gross breach of the therapeutic relationship and that predicting violence with certainty is highly questionable. The courts rejected these arguments, but the issues are by no means straightforward, as anyone who has counseled persons about their problems knows.

Suffice it to say that pastors are limited by their own obligation to society and by the requirement to protect persons from harming themselves or others. No pastor can take refuge in the statement, "I only deal with spiritual matters." A pastor is a member of society and lives in this world as well as the next. As Everstine et al. suggest (about psychologists):

> As a result of this kind of thinking, the therapist may be drawn into a double-bind situation in which he or she is (a) damned if the client is not provided with help to overcome violent tendencies and (b) damned if the violent tendencies are not reported to "proper authorities."[3]

This double bind is not confined to psychologists. Pastors experience it too.

Two other issues regarding the limits of confidentiality should be mentioned. The first has to do with whether or not the person can order the pastor to reveal a confidence. In the case of the psychiatrist who went to jail rather than reveal a confidence, the court ruled that the client rather than the doctor held the power to end the confidence. This is true for physicians, attorneys, psychologists, and accountants but may not be true for ministers. They hold the power to withhold information shared with them in confidence *even if* the parishioner waives the right to secrecy. No legal power can force a minister to reveal a confidence if the rules of the minister's church require that it be kept secret. Ministers are the only professionals who have this right. Others must testify if ordered to by the court or if confidentiality is waived by the client. It is important to note that this privilege applies only where the explicit rules of the church specify that their ministers have a duty to keep information secret. If the church rules do not state this, a minister may be required to breach confidentiality. However, this is not usually the case. Courts typically honor a pastor's refusal to testify.

The second issue has to do with the breadth of confidentiality for which pastors are responsible. Here they are most like family physicians, who are concerned for the total health of their patients, not just the symptoms that may accompany a specific complaint. As Everstine et al. noted, most physicians assume a "duty of silence" in regard to their patients and agree with that portion of the Hippocratic oath which states, "Whatever in connection with my profession, or not in connection with it, I may see or hear in the lives of men which ought not to be spoken abroad I will not divulge as reckoning that all should be kept silent."[4] Pastors, like physicians, assume a lifelong, broad, interpersonal, and familial responsibility for persons. Thus, they should treat all that they hear as confidential, because by divulging it they may endanger or make more difficult the lives of those entrusted to their care.

This is a much broader concern than most other professionals assume in regard to those with whom they work. It also makes the keeping of confidences a much more serious issue, because much that a pastor hears is not in a private office but is communicated as the pastor fulfills the day-to-day parish duties of ministry and administration.

The Several Settings of Pastoral Confidentiality

We have said that the vocation of pastor includes functions that differ from those of the typical professional who deals with persons. A comparison with one of these, the psychologist, illustrates this point.

Function	Psychologist	Minister
Preacher		X
Pastor		X
Teacher	maybe	X
Administrator	maybe	X
Consultant	X	maybe
Diagnostician	X	
Counselor	X	X
Researcher	maybe	
Writer	maybe	maybe
Colleague	X	X
Confidant		X
Friend		X
Family member	X	X

The list is not meant to be exhaustive, but it can easily be seen that the minister is involved with people in more unofficial and casual but nevertheless essential ways than is the psychologist. Comparisons with other helping professionals would reveal similar relationships.

This means that the pastors carry a much wider range of contacts and are privy to much more information about the lives of persons than are other professionals. Not only is there more and varied information communicated but the possibilities for sharing that information in interactions are greatly increased. It is one thing to go from one's office to home and back with occasional contacts over the phone with other professionals, and quite another thing to sit with a family member during an operation, attend a women's luncheon, counsel a troubled family, and plan next year's budget all in the same day! For example, the professional psychologist may sit in a controlled office setting and speak to others about narrowly defined professional matters, after which it is possible to go home to a leisurely supper followed by a relaxed evening with the family. On the other hand, the pastor may not relax until after 10:00 P.M., after switching roles at least four times during the day. This is not an easy task, and what is or is not permissible to share in these several settings may become blurred in the process.

As was noted earlier, pastors are most like family physicians in assuming an overarching concern for the general welfare of those with whom they deal. At the very least, pastors implicitly share with physicians the Hippocratic admonition to do no harm even if they cannot be of help. However, even here it is apparent that, in comparison, the roles of the physician are more limited and that they are expressed within a controlled office situation.

A full list of the types of situations where pastoral confidentiality might be violated would be extensive. The descriptions that follow will illustrate dilemmas pastors often face. "What should they reveal and to whom?"—this is the question.

When the pastor refers someone to a counselor

When the counselor asks for background information

When the pastor and counselor work with the same person

When a lawyer requests information in a divorce or child custody case

When informing new staff members about the persons with whom they will be working

When giving illustrations in a sermon

When telling newcomers about the church

When training lay counselors or church visitors

When handling administrative problems such as choosing leaders or dealing with ineffectiveness

When resolving disputes between church members

When told about misbehavior in church members ranging from peccadilloes to major offenses

When a church leader is divorced or is accused of immorality

When dealing with families at births, weddings, illness, transitions, deaths

When writing letters or a column for newspaper or church newsletter

When keeping pastoral records

When leaving the church and sharing with the new pastor what to expect from certain persons

When talking with a fellow pastor

When talking with family or spouse

When told something by or about church officials that would harm their effectiveness

When giving advice over the phone

Many other situations could be added to this list. Finding one's way through these complex relationships and feeling that one has not violated confidences or harmed others is a little like wending one's way through a maze with five alternatives at each turn! However, there are some guidelines to help ministers in these endeavors.

Guidelines for Keeping Pastoral Confidences

The first guideline is personal rather than professional. As far as possible, ministers should keep their personal lives separate from their professional roles. Although this is impossible in an absolute sense, it, nevertheless, should be a goal toward which ministers aspire, because if they don't they will find themselves using information defensively or manipulatively. For example, one minister was displeased with his house. He encouraged the church to purchase a better one for him. Some in the congregation supported him while others did not. He got angry with his opponents and shared with some of his supporters the rumor that one of the people who disagreed with him was having an affair with the organist. What a misuse of information! Without question, it did harm far beyond the anger it evoked from the people involved. This is not to say that the couple should not have been confronted, but the way in which the pastor used the information mixed his personal feelings with his professional role. Too often ministers confuse their own feelings of self-worth with whether persons support a program they have planned. Getting too much invested in one's own ideas can easily give rise to that sort of unfortunate situation.

Another aspect of this matter is the personal life of the minister. In earlier days the minister was called the "parson"—literally, person—*the* one in the community to whom others looked for example and integrity. While today that may be too high an expectation, it is still important for the minister to be as well adjusted and free from conflict as possible. Of course, this includes keeping his or her own spiritual development alive and growing. To the extent that ministers are happily married and mentally healthy, they can better manage the knowledge they have of others in the labyrinth of roles involved in ministry. This is part of the genius inherent in the admonitions of 1 Timothy 3, where the writer details the characteristics to seek in those who desire to become bishops and deacons. Apart from the moral implications of these characteristics, there is the dynamic reality that one can function better if one's personal life is intact.

If a pastor intends to use in preaching or writing an illustration based on actual events, prior permission to use the information should be obtained from the persons involved. It does not matter whether or not the event occurred in a previous parish, nor does it matter that one changes the conditions to safeguard the identity of the persons. There may be, and often are, persons in the congregation who know the other parish and can make the identification. Again, people often know when preachers are disguising information and can make transpositions which allow them to identify the persons being described. One minister's wife, for example, said she always knew when he spoke to think east when he said west, male when he said female. In all cases, the issues should be cleared with those whose story is being used.

This is not only an ethical matter, it is also a professional and legal matter having to do with the best care for persons and the possibility that one can be sued if an individual has not given permission. Everstine et al. report a case in which two mental health professionals lost a suit involving their use of a client's case in a book in spite of the fact that they had disguised the identity. The court ruled that confidentiality had been breached because prior consent to use the information had not been given.[5] Pastors could be held to be liable in the same manner.

Although obtaining prior permission may involve extra effort, it will be experienced by people as genuine concern and will result in more effective ministry.

Written consent should be obtained for the use of any information that is to printed—even if only as duplicated sermons for dispersal within the congregation. The consent form should include the following details:

1. What information is to be used

2. Where and under what conditions it is to be used

3. For how long the permission is granted

4. How the person may revoke the permission

5. What the pastor will do if she or he desires to use the information in any other way and at any other time

Although these details may seem overly specific, they nevertheless indicate full respect for the privacy and the rights of the individual and communicate a genuine concern by the pastor not to abuse the trust of others. Further, they will protect the pastor from legal action.

Without question, such a signed statement should be requested from those who ask a pastor to testify in any court trial or from those a pastor has referred to another professional, such as a psychiatrist, psychologist, or physician.

Care in such matters will strengthen the bonds between pastor and parishioner, protect everyone from embarrassment, and help keep all concerned out of legal complications.

7

Insurance Protection for Church and Clergy

Thomas L. Needham

The recent expansion of church and clergy liability into the costly areas of malpractice, sexual abuse of children, and sexual misconduct have increased losses for insurers. The actual dollar amounts, the number of cases, and the relation of these figures to those in other professions is not known at this time. Like churches, insurance companies did not anticipate the recent legal developments. It is possible that some companies may develop strategies to deal with any anticipated financial drain of the unexpected legal decisions.

This is an important time for churches, clergy, and insurance companies to understand each other and work together. Without a reversal of this litigious trend, churches may have to allocate ever larger percentages of their church budgets for insurance premiums or face the necessity of operating with reduced or eliminated coverage. This chapter can assist churches and clergy in understanding and protecting their coverage through the following considerations: (1) the role of church insurance in risk shifting, (2) the self-perpetuating nature of risk shifting, (3) the increasing role of insurance in the church, (4) new challenges to church insurers, (5) how insurance companies are fighting back, and (6) how to protect insurance protection.

The Role of Church Insurance in Risk Shifting

What does the insurer provide church and clergy? While the answers vary with changing times, insurance makes two general provisions for risk shifting. At the legal and financial level, insurance provides for the financial risks of legal defense and of settlements or judgments. At the psychological level, it provides for the psychological risk that one's personal error or some unforeseen circumstance could reduce or eliminate the church through costly legal defense, settlements, or judgments.

The risks churches and clergy have shifted to insurance companies are constantly changing. The liability policies of today are quite different from the policies of fifty years ago, because the scope of coverage in general church liability has changed in accordance with the increased legal vulnerability of church and clergy. In its early form, church liability insurance covered damage to property, personal injury, and death. However, the reimbursement was limited to actual damages. In recent years, as the church has succumbed to the general legal climate in America, church insurers have necessarily included liability coverage for pain and suffering, punitive damages, and emotional distress. This continual expansion of liability, with the subsequent expansion of insurance coverage, both within a short period of time, has had great financial impact.[1]

Within the context of an expanding litigious climate, church insurers have developed various strategies to ensure their financial longevity and their ability to provide insurance for church and clergy. These measures include offering additional policies for clergy malpractice and lay counseling. Before discussing important developments like these, the self-perpetuating nature of risk shifting will be explored.

The Self-perpetuating Nature of Risk Shifting

The shifting of risk to government is necessary for the protection of the victim, just as the shifting of risk to insurance companies is necessary for the protection of an individual or organization's financial future. Nonetheless, both necessary risk shifting trends accelerate risk occurrences; the former through fostering the idea of government intervention, the latter through facilitating carelessness.

The first self-perpetuating aspect of risk shifting is the no-risk mentality that has evolved with the consumer protection movement. As was discussed in chapter 1, this movement was closely linked to the rapid industrialization and urbanization that began after the Civil War. With the manufacturing of products removed from the small local business community to remote and inaccessible locations, individuals were thwarted in their replacement of faulty merchandise. This meant that the purchasing of goods involved a risk in both quality and serviceability. Consumers, then and now, have been more and more unwilling to assume the risk of faulty purchases. The central consumer concerns became "How can my risks be reduced or eliminated?" and "Who can make this happen?"

The answer was found in government regulation. Yair Aharoni, author of *The No-Risk Society*, describes how in America, as in all developed countries, the government is the entity to which risk is being shifted. So frequent is this shift that Aharoni speaks of it as a new social order:

> A new social order has evolved that started with a reliance by citizens on government for the solution to certain economic, social and cultural problems and has grown to include pressures on government to mitigate almost every risk any individual might be asked to bear.[2]

This new social order made rapid advances following World War II, the time that Aharoni calls the "no-risk" period. The rationale became one in which every individual was to be protected from the consequences of almost all personal disaster,

> was to be insured, not only against unemployment, but also against an ever growing array of untoward events. Consumers were insured against faulty products, victims against criminals, property owners against acts of nature, drug manufacturers against misconcocted serums, depositors against bank loss, lenders against mortgage defaults. About the only group that was not insured were the believers in governmental omnipotence.[3]

As an activated social force, protectionism continues to expand by generating new agendas for public concern. Now the church and clergy have been added to the agenda and may occasionally find their ministry the focus of public debate and judicial review. It is possible that either churches or plaintiffs against churches will eventually appeal to the U.S. Supreme Court for clarification on the limits of church and clergy liability.

The second self-perpetuating aspect of risk shifting is what the insurance industry calls the "moral hazard." This is a term coined to describe the increased carelessness that results from being insured. After the insured has transferred specified financial risks there is a tendency to be less cautious and take fewer preventive efforts. This tendency may be further exacerbated for some churches who believe that their First Amendment protection gives them absolute immunity from liability.

Clergy and church may not be able to extricate themselves from the first self-perpetuating aspect of risk shifting and increased litigation, but they can take preventive measures to avoid carelessness, the moral hazard. This is especially important today, considering the recent attention to the liability of the church and the uncertainty of the ultimate extent of past, present, and future liability.

The Increasing Role of Insurance in the Church

There was a time when churches and clergy did not need insurance. However, as the new social order has activated government regulations to expand the liability of church and clergy, the role of insurance companies has necessarily increased.

According to Church Mutual's John Cleary, the legal vulnerability of the church has emerged slowly. Over the past fifty years, laws that had previously prohibited litigation against churches and charitable institutions began to change, so that now "no state has charitable immunity for churches or religious institutions."[4] This increasing involvement in the adversary tort system has prompted insurance carriers to provide church liability coverage.[5]

Until the mid-seventies, churches secured their liability coverage from church specialty companies like Preferred Risk Mutual Insurance Group, Church Mutual Insurance Company, and Brotherhood because general insurance companies were usually not interested in providing church coverage. Their interest and availability changed, however, when, in the late sixties, interest rates soared and insurance companies were forced to seek new ways of generating monies.

The commercial marketplace, which includes churches, Christian schools, and religious organizations, became an attractive source from which the general insurance companies sought to generate premiums quickly. They were able to attract churches with low premiums, which they were actually writing at a loss, believing that the high interest rates of the late 1970s would offset the losses in claims. The current industry-wide insurance crisis has resulted because this risky practice failed.

Insurance companies now seek to restabilize their financial reserves by withdrawing from certain insurance markets and raising premiums in others.[6] Nearly thirty companies withdrew from the church insurance market in the first half of 1985. But what is more important is that some of the old standard church specialty insurance companies are expanding into other markets while reducing their concentration in church insurance. One specialty carrier will not renew 50 percent of its insured churches. According to Jack Kelly, Preferred Risk's Director of Commercial Marketing, "Since 1984 unanticipated suits against churches and Christian schools have piled up with a vengeance."

New Challenges to Church Insurers

The contemporary challenges to church insurance will be faced by the remaining general insurance companies and the church specialty companies, such as Church Mutual, Preferred Risk, and Brotherhood.

Preferred Risk, the largest insurer of churches and charitable organizations, reports dramatic increases in the volume of litigation as well as in the growing number of new types of claims.

> Preferred Risk has over 25,000 such organizations insured. Religious institutions have definitely been experiencing a dramatic increase in the number of lawsuits brought against them as well as in the size of the settlements being requested and often awarded. Claims are now arising out of issues which have previously not been faced by churches.[7]

Al Davidson, Vice-President of Claims for Brotherhood, reports that while his company remains committed to the church market, they must now contend with the increasing volume and cost of current claims. According to Davidson there are two primary factors causing insurance companies to take dramatic action. The first factor is the unnecessary claim: "The number of catastrophes in the church is too high!" The second factor is the loss of public respect and legal immunity: "Today, people are just as quick to sue the church as a secular organization." While experiencing an increasing volume of litigation, Church Mutual has not experienced big losses with the new types of liability in malpractice and sexual misconduct.

Church Mutual's corporate attorney, John Cleary, reports an increase in new types of cases, but without severe losses. Since 1979, nearly 15 malpractice-type cases have been filed against their insured churches. At the time of publication several of these cases were pending but most had been dismissed, some had gone to trial, but no verdicts or settlements had been paid.[8]

Cleary anticipates that the frequency of malpractice cases will slowly increase, but he does not expect that Church Mutual will pay large verdicts or settlements in the near future.

In a recent highly informative booklet, Preferred Risk tells churches and charitable organizations about their experience with dramatic increases in the number of suits and in the size of settlements and awards, and about the new types of claims being filed. The following excerpt from this booklet demonstrates the breadth of litigation against many churches and clergy.

1. Liability without physical injury
   Libel and slander
   Public demonstrations against individuals, groups, or organizations if improperly conducted
   Discharge of students or expulsion of members of congregations
   Invasion of privacy
   Publication of accusations
   Counseling by insufficiently trained or unskilled counselors

2. Accidents that occur during improper supervision

3. Grounds and building liability, such as lighting, handrails, fire exit signs

4. Hazardous activities, such as water slides, basketball, hay rides

5. Bus ministry liability, caused by improper maintenance of buses, poorly trained drivers, or lack of safety equipment (fire extinguishers, first-aid kits)

6. Hiring and employment practices, such as nondiscriminatory policies, and proper termination procedures

7. Sexual misconduct, including molestation[9]

The high cost of the unanticipated malpractice and child-abuse suits has caused some insurance companies to feel uneasy about the extent to which they will have to deplete reserve accounts. Insurance companies establish the rate of today's policies on tomorrow's projected losses. But as Preferred's Jack Kelly says, the challenge today is to pay the unanticipated high losses of malpractice and child abuse on yesterday's premiums based on anticipated fires, slips, and falls.

Regardless of whether or not there is a settlement or verdict in these unanticipated new kinds of suits, the defense costs can be high. While Church Mutual currently pays only $3,000 to $5,000 defense costs for a malpractice suit, Preferred Risk paid $250,000 in defense costs for Grace Community Church, and the pending appeal to the California Supreme Court will result in additional expense. Preferred's Vice-President of Claims, Robert Plunk, says that the high cost of defense proves that "you can be totally right and still spend a million dollars in defending a case."

Settlements and court awards are also mounting. Again, Church Mutual reports an increase in claims of sexual misconduct or abuse against all types of church employees, including clergy. But these claims have not resulted in significant losses either in defense costs, settlements, or verdicts. Preferred Risk, however, reports dramatic increases in claims of sexual misconduct and abuse against clergy and church employees, Christian school teachers and employees, and Christian school students. Defense costs, settlements, and awards range from $50,000 to $1,000,000 per case.

Insurance companies are also being challenged by the way some churches and clergy conduct their ministries. They confront the legal vulnerabilities of extreme religious practices or poorly selected clergy or church employees. In one such case, a court awarded a woman $300,000 and assigned the $75,-000 in legal fees to the church insurer, because a member of her congregation tried to beat demons out of her with a stick. One case involving several sexual abuse victims was settled for $4,000,000. In another sexual abuse case, a teenage student with a rare form of venereal disease penetrated 60 to 90 elementary-school girls, all in a Christian school. In a pending suit, a woman alleges her minister raped her after inducing a hypnotic state. Add to this the litigation for bus accidents, slips, and falls, and insurance companies have encountered a growing challenge within the religious community.

Furthermore, now that the courts have expanded church liability, including cases where the statutes of limitations are being discarded, many church insurers have been confronted with almost unlimited liability. Because they did not anticipate the new types of claims for malpractice, sexual misconduct, and abuse, they did not predict the need to limit their liability in these areas. A policy written today restricts the insurance company's liability to $1,000,000 *per occurrence*. If sexual abuse is alleged and proven, even if it involves 100 children, the maximum liability of the insurer is $1,000,000. However, a case of sexual abuse involving as many as 60 to 90 children could cost insurance companies as much as $1,000,000 *per child,* because the policies were written at a time when no one comprehended the potential of legal and financial vulnerability to church and clergy.

How Insurance Companies Are Fighting Back

Insurance companies that continue underwriting churches and religious organizations are protecting themselves through various combinations of defensive strategies: (1) educational strategies, (2) increased premiums and decreased coverage, (3) selective underwriting, (4) aggregate limits, (5) professional requirements and restrictions, (6) exclusion clauses, and (7) special policies.

Educational Strategies

Insurance companies agree that prevention is the best policy. They seek to help their insureds reduce the probability of lawsuits by providing information through filmstrips, seminars and lectures, booklets, and free consultations. Most companies also provide legal counsel to their insured churches and clergy to assist them in making critical decisions and avoiding common pitfalls.

Church insurers expressed interest in books such as this one as an aid in helping churches reduce litigation. Some indicated they are planning workshops designed to help clergy recognize individuals needing referral to a mental health professional because they are mentally ill or suicidal. Many insurers have already provided this type of training in the recognition of alcoholism.

Increased Premiums and Decreased Coverage

Can liability and malpractice insurance escalate for clergy as it has for professionals? Yes it can! In its educational booklet, Preferred Risk, the largest church carrier, wrote: "Church premiums will escalate at unprecedented rates unless appropriate action is taken to reverse this litigious trend."[10] According to Preferred's Robert Plunk, this means that prices will go up at the same time that coverage will go down. In part this results from the previously discussed high cost of defense.

Selective Underwriting

All insurance companies must make a decision as to whether or not they will underwrite (insure) a particular individual or organization. In 1985, many secular organizations lost their insurance. The Rapid Transit District of Southern California and 6,500 lawyers in the Los Angeles Bar Association were among the increasing number of those finding it difficult to secure an underwriter.[11] Insurance companies, church specialty insurers included, have begun to reassess the future of church insurance. As we have seen, many companies have already reduced or eliminated church insurance because of unanticipated losses in the religious community. Without appropriate measures, many more churches could find themselves in this predicament.

Aggregate Limits

Preferred's Director of Commercial Marketing, Jack Kelly, says that, unlike previous policies, new and renewed policies will specify aggregate limits. For example, if the policy limits are $300,000 and $1,000,000, then in the case of child abuse, the policy would provide a maximum coverage of $300,000 per occurrence and an aggregate limit of $1,000,000 for all occurrences. The limit would apply regardless of the number of people involved. Unlike claims being filed under previous policies, a sexual abuse suit would no longer cost up to $1,000,000 per child.

Professional Requirements and Restrictions

In order for a pastor's counseling and professional duties to be covered by a general liability policy, most insurers require the minister to be ordained and functioning within the scope of pastoral duties. According to Robert Plunk, Preferred Risk has additional stipulations of seminary graduation and six units of either undergraduate or graduate counselor training. There will be fewer exceptions to these requirements in future, with only a limited number going to seasoned clergy without a history of previous counseling problems.

Further requirements that will begin to figure into Preferred's decision to insure a church or pastor will include a positive attitude toward psychiatric or psychological referral, the promotion of pastoral counseling within one's church rather than to the community at large, and the limiting of pastoral counseling to the scope of pastoral duties.

Exclusion Clauses

Another way that insurance companies will fight back is to write policies that exclude certain activities. Sexual misconduct or abuse and lay counseling are two such examples. Most insurance companies typically exclude not only the cost of settlements or awards but also the cost of legal defense in sexual abuse or misconduct suits.

Church Mutual has been an exception to the typical sexual exclusion clause, inasmuch as they pay the cost of legal defense until their defendant is clearly guilty. Preferred Risk has been one of the few companies that has provided full coverage for sexual misconduct or abuse. However, as they renew church policies, all future coverage will be excluded. Vice-President Plunk says their final draft of the exclusion will read something like this: "any actual or alleged sexual misconduct will not be covered or defended."

Lay counseling is another common exclusion. Neither Church Mutual nor Brotherhood include this coverage in their general liability policies. Preferred Risk, on the other hand, includes lay counseling as a part of its general liability policy.

Special Policies

Additional insurance can be secured for both the ministers' professional duties and for lay counseling. While malpractice is generally covered in the church's general liability policy, some companies, such as Church Mutual, offer separate malpractice policies for clergy. In the event a given defense, settlement or award exceeds the general liability coverage, the clergy who purchase this malpractice insurance have additional coverage and security.

Since lay counseling is not covered by most general church liability policies, churches that wish coverage of their ministry must secure separate insurance. Surplus lines companies, such as the Great American Surplus Lines Insurance Company in

Pasadena, California, offer coverage for those kinds of activities not included on general liability policies or by special policies. This coverage is considered high risk, and premiums are established accordingly. The Pasadena company provides lay counseling coverage at an annual premium of approximately $800 per person.

How to Protect Insurance Protection

Appropriate actions need to be taken to protect insurance protection. Churches and clergy can cooperate with insurance companies in developing aggressive measures to counter increasing litigation. These efforts could protect premium costs, further reduction in coverage, and possibly insurability. The grim alternatives are already being faced by some businesses and corporations in Southern California. If these same kinds of alternatives were forced upon church and clergy, they would have to absorb increases in insurance premiums by allocating more of the church budget to insurance premiums, go without coverage, stay out of certain types of ministries, or close up shop.[12]

While this entire volume focuses upon ways to reduce liability and thereby protect one's insurance, there are five specific precautionary measures worth noting: (1) clarify your protection, (2) develop preventive strategies, (3) adhere to an ethical standard of care, (4) don't add insult to injury, and (5) cooperate with your insurance company.

1. Clarify Your Protection

The adaptive quality of church liability coverage has been discussed in this chapter. However, there are some areas, such as the mixing of psychological counseling with pastoral duties, that may result in unexpected liability exposure to church or clergy. Below you will find a type of question that may spur you on to further clarification of your church and clergy insurance needs. It is suggested that you develop a list of questions and concerns and then seek answers from your church's legal counsel as well as your insurance carrier.

The following questions have been answered by three major church insurers relative to their general church liability policy coverage. The question is: Are these covered areas of ministry?

	Brother-hood	Church Mutual	Pre-ferred Risk
Psychotherapy performed by a pastor who is also a state-licensed therapist?	Yes	No	Yes
Pastoral counseling within the scope of spiritual guidance?	Yes	Yes	Yes
Church counseling centers, with state-licensed counselors, charging fees?	No	No	Yes
Lay counseling ministry?	No	No	Yes
Expulsion from church through public disclosure of private facts?	Yes	Yes	Yes

2. Develop Preventive Strategies

Churches and clergy are being forced to confront the vulnerability of a complex legal world. They must learn how to navigate through the troubled areas of individual rights.

First, church and clergy must learn about individuals' rights to confidentiality. Gossip, prayer requests, and group discussions about the efficacy of other persons' actions could be grounds for an invasion-of-privacy suit. Lawsuits have been threatened against churches that have made an individual's unsaved condition a matter of public prayer. Lay counselors or pastoral counselors who reveal information given in confidence have also violated individuals' rights.

Second, church and clergy need to become more realistic about the psychological problems of many laity and clergy. Becoming a Christian is not a cure either for moral problems or for psychological ones. Yet the burden of wanting to be "acceptable" to God often leads to the denial of problems that will only intensify because they are submerged.

Third, church and clergy must remove the spiritual fear and stigma associated with seeking professional help. This is an essential part of providing hope and change for many troubled Christians.

3. Adhere to an Ethical Standard of Care

In the Appendix, the reader will find ethical statements from the American Association for Marriage and Family Therapy, the American Association of Pastoral Counselors, the American Psychological Association, and the Christian Association for Psychological Studies. These standards have been developed to maintain the quality of care provided individuals.

When professionals are confronted with litigation, the courts want answers to several questions: Was another professional consulted? Was the defendant professional operating within the boundaries of his or her training and experience? How standardized and acceptable was the treatment rendered? When widely accepted ethical standards are adhered to, professionals weather the legal assaults.

4. Don't Add Insult to Injury

If someone alleges a wrongdoing against church or clergy, it should be taken seriously. One should not be argumentative or hostile. Rather, one should be receptive and reassuring that everything possible will be done to correct the wrongs. Following this encounter, and before any further conversations, the pastor or a church representative should contact both the church's and the insurer's attorneys.

5. Cooperate with Your Insurance Company

In the event of a lawsuit, insurance companies need the complete cooperation of both church and clergy for the preparation of the best defense. This means that a full disclosure of information must be made to the attorneys, and ultimately to the court.

What if the church wants the insurer to settle out of court? Insurance companies reserve the right to make the final decision about whether or not a particular case should be taken to court. As Preferred's corporate attorney says, every effort is made to consider the request of the church, but the final decision does rest with the insurance company.

8

The Future of Ministry in a Changing World

H. Newton Malony

In his book *Today's Pastor in Tomorrow's World,* Carnegie Samuel Calian examines eight models of ministry: the servant-shepherd, the politician-prophet, the preacher-teacher, the evangelist-charismatic, the pragmatist-promoter, the manager-enabler, the liturgist-celebrant, and specialized ministries such as those that involve counseling of various types.[1] He sees particular promise in this last type of ministry, and it is to such ministries that the issues of malpractice discussed in this book apply. If indeed such ministries continue to grow in importance, there will be even greater need to give careful attention to situations in which charges of malpractice might be leveled.

Other styles, however, will not be immune to problems.

The baptism of "baby Faye," the child given a baboon heart, raises the issue of the quality of service afforded by the priest who administered the sacrament. The parents wanted to be present at the service but discovered that the priest had come unannounced, baptized the baby, and left a calling card. If the news reports of this incident are accurate, the quality of service was probably significantly below that which the priest would normally have given. Standards of care will become of increasing concern in the future.

A parallel illustration relates to the difficulty sufferers from AIDS and their families have encountered when they have sought pastoral service. AIDS is simply the latest example of the difficulty ministers have experienced in ministering to those who were "dying with stigma." Leprosy, gonorrhea, and alcoholism were earlier situations which tested the intent of ministers to provide loving care without judgment—a standard that physicians have espoused since the time of Hippocrates. As Alastair Campbell has suggested in his insightful book on professional care, it is highly questionable whether the service given by professional helpers should be called "love." When love breaks down, as seems to have been the case in some pastoral care of AIDS victims, love loses its meaning and deteriorates into self-serving reciprocity. More harm than good is done when the expectation of love is disappointed. Better that care should be judged by "justice" than by "love." Then one could call ministers to task when they refused to care for those dying with stigma because they would be refusing to give that which any individual deserved just for being human—regardless of why they were in a certain situation.

Yet another situation illustrates a recurring difficulty in the preaching-teaching role of ministry. *Time* magazine reported in 1984 that a member of a church in Oklahoma had an affair with the mayor of the town.[2] Although both were divorced, the fact that they had sexual intercourse was judged by the elders of the church to be fornication—a sin which they felt required confession and censure. The woman confessed her error to the elders but refused to confess her sin publicly. They told her she would have to openly acknowledge her error before the congregation in order to remain a member. She resigned from the church. The elders, in turn, announced her sin and condemned her even though she was no longer a member of the church. She sued the church for invasion of privacy. The conviction of the church that it had to expose sin conflicted with the rights of the individual to a life lived apart from public scrutiny.

A related example of how ministers will continue to be subjected to malpractice issues pertains to the manager-enabler role. A church secretary was accused of dealing in drugs. At her trial the minister of the church was called to the stand to testify about her character *as his secretary*. The prosecutor asked him whether they had discussed the drug charges and what had been said. He refused to answer on the grounds that his sole role was to testify about her character as her employer and that conversations he might have had with her were confidential. The judge sentenced him to jail until he testified. He was later released. However, the event illustrates the difficulty ministers will have in the future in maintaining the age old pastor-penitent privilege in a justice-conscious society. The responsibility of society to convict criminals and the rights of persons to confidential conversations with ministers will become even more difficult to mediate.

A final example of future malpractice issues can be seen in the majority judgment ruling against summary dismissal of the suit against Grace Community Church. In their ruling, the judges said that if a manual used in the training of church counselors stated that killing yourself was one way a sinner could go home to God, then the church possibly would be responsible if a guilt-prone client committed suicide. The judges said this was an issue that should be tried, so they ruled that the case should come to court. Seemingly the church would be responsible if it could be proved that its counselors used the teaching about suicide and communicated permission to their client to kill himself. The church's claim that such teaching was never communicated to the young man leaves it vulnerable at best, since its manual included such statements, whether they be taken out of context or not. Here is an example of a conflict between the ideals of society that individual life may not be ended intentionally and the teachings of a religious body. Although the statements in the manual may seem outlandish to some, they illustrate many issues where church and state may have different answers to the problems people face.

Professionalism

Let us return, however, to a discussion of the tent-making specialized style which Calian feels will increasingly characterize ministry in the future. One of the inevitable characteristics of specialization is a tendency toward professionalism. Although ministry has been thought to be one of the oldest professions, professionalism as such is a recent phenomenon. This can be seen clearly in the development of the American Association of Pastoral Counselors, which began as an interest group for parish pastors but which has become an association of independent practitioners who function apart from the local church, in spite of the fact that they are required to be ordained in some denomination and often are on the staff of church-related counseling centers. Dues for active membership are as high, or higher, than those for psychologists, optometrists, dentists, and marriage counselors in similar organizations. They have hierarchies of membership based on competence demonstrated before their own committees, and they exert pressure for recognition on insurance companies and state governments. They function as a profession in the current meaning of that term—as a group of trained persons who have knowledge or skill to "profess," who function independently of institutional control, and who regulate themselves through ethical standards and professional committees.

Professions in our culture are problematic at best. Most of them offer service to the public. Attorneys, physicians, and social workers are examples, along with specialized ministers. In most cases professions are help-giving, so that the misfortunes of others are the occasion of their services. Thus, their function inevitably brings into question their motivation. Are they primarily concerned with service or with personal advantage? In a somewhat cynical comment on this question, Alastair Campbell said, "There is, at least, an ambiguity and, at worst, a deep dishonesty in the notion of professional care. Other people's ill health, confusion, and social disadvantage are sources of power, status and income for those groups in society who offer their services as professional helpers. What then are we to make of the high-sounding ethical codes of such self-styled 'caring professions'?"[3] Are these codes of conduct ways of protecting the public from inept practitioners or ways of protecting the advantage of the profession from those who might offer equal service but are not members of the "guild"?

Guild concerns may make more sense in plumbing than in counseling. The latter is a role that has been exercised by friends and sages throughout the centuries without cost and with marked skill. Is limiting it to professionals a way of guaranteeing quality of service or, rather, of protecting the status of certain persons? These will be important questions for those in specialized ministries to continue to ask themselves in the future.

In return for guarantees by the state that they can have a monopoly on carrying out their prescribed tasks, that they can limit the number of persons entering the profession, that they can control entry into the profession by prescribing training and performance, and that they can control when and where their tasks are undertaken, professions promise their commitment to the common good, their trustworthiness, their willingness to guarantee a standard of service, and their intent to discipline their own membership.[4] These are complex and interrelated sets of assumptions. There is no such thing as pure motivation. "Professional" ministry in the future will continually need to examine itself regarding its intentions and its performance.

Recent trends in the church and in the training of clergy are away from professionalism and toward the training of laity for many types of counseling which have been traditionally under clergy control. In addition, the emphasis on spiritual direction may or may not include the training and specialization of professional counselors.

Yet the statement is still true; typically, parish pastors and staff who serve religious organizations are protected from accusations about the quality of their performance in a way that freestanding professions are not. Professionals have no one to fall back on save themselves. If their service does not match the quality guaranteed by their professional ethics, they can have their licenses removed and can be prevented from practicing.

Standard of Care

In the future, as the services of many more ministers are called into question, both the quality and the quantity of care will be challenged. Quality has to do with "what" is provided, while quantity pertains to the "amount." Both quality and quantity refer to what has come to be known as "standard of care."

Before considering these issues in more detail, let us say that ministerial "standard of care" is peculiarly vulnerable in light of the religious tradition that ordained ministers mediate the love of God to human beings by their words and by their actions. This lays on ministry a type of expectation that goes beyond the technical skill of physicians and attorneys, for example. Love is hard to measure and the perennial questions have been "Where does sacrificial love begin and end?" and "Does love include action in behalf of justice as well as empathy in behalf of support?" If love is the standard for ministry, then the arena for challenge becomes great indeed.

Quality of Care

What quality of service does professional ministry promise? This is equal to asking, "What makes the service of ministry unique?" Much has been written on this issue. Without doubt the counsel given by ministers has often been indistinguishable from that given by other professional therapists. From one point of view, this is as it should be. Ministers should evidence no less skill in basic counseling techniques than other professionals of like training. Ours is a day in which much is known about human experience and the ways to best assure rapport and confidence in a relationship.

However, ministers claim to represent a perspective that is not automatically a part of other professional viewpoints, and it is this perspective that is sometimes missing in the counsel given by ministers. In a situation known to us, a pastoral counselor gave a series of talks at a local church attended by one of his counselees. In his talks he discussed the religious dimensions of certain human problems. After the talks were over the counselee said, "Why didn't you ever share some of these ideas in our sessions?" The pastoral counselor had to admit to himself that he had left this "religious" dimension out of his professional counseling and that what he did was probably indistinguishable from that offered by nonreligious counselors in the same city.

Since ministers are considered to be mediators of God, people have a right to expect that their professional service will include this dimension. Don Browning affirms this in the title, as well as the content, of his book *The Moral Context of Pastoral Care*.[5] Likewise, Jürgen Moltmann supports this contention by his assertion that all pastoral care should be permeated with a dimension of Christian hope.[6] Halmos contends that belief in the triumph of sacrificial love—agape—is the core component of the faith of the Christian counselor.[7]

Ministry in the future may not only need continually to remind itself of this transcendent dimension which justifies its existence among the professions, it may also need to remind those who utilize its services that this type of service will be offered. Many persons come to pastors for counsel solely because the pastors are available and because they are free. They do not expect spiritual counsel. One pastor who is aware of this tendency always starts his counseling by asking, "Are you aware of what building this is and who I am?" He seeks to remind them that his office is in a church and that he is a minister. Perhaps in the future it will be helpful for pastors to put into print what they will be doing with those who come to them for help. Psychoanalysts would not want to be misperceived. Ministers should desire no less.

Another aspect of quality control has to do with the tension between love and justice. A psychoanalyst may get away with not dealing with the environment of the analysand, but can the minister? Is not justice as essential a component of ministerial concern as is adjustment and acceptance? The testimony of the eighth-century prophets and the witness of such contemporary movements as the social gospel and liberation theology seem to suggest that justice is at the center of the Christian message —a message which ministers embody. Judgment as well as grace is essential for ministry to be Christian. There must be moral confrontation in counseling, as Browning notes. There must be moral confrontation with society, as Statham notes.[8] Likewise there must be grace offered to both the individual and to society. Both persons and cultures come under God's judgment and love. Future ministry which does not include both emphases may deserve criticism for its lack of quality control.

Yet another qualitative issue with which future ministry must deal is its understanding of the goals toward which its service is directed. In light of the above discussion of the transcendent and moral dimensions, it will no longer suffice for ministry to espouse or parrot culture's view on the goals of counseling—whether they are expressed in psychological or physical terms. In a penetrating survey of how the goals of pastoral care have changed over the last several centuries, Holifield observed that the understanding of what made for happiness has been shaped by politics, science, and cultural achievements as well as theological developments. He noted that mid-twentieth-century pastoral theologians have been interested in "correlating" the emphases between theology and psychology. This has resulted in a too-facile "equation of self-realization and spiritual growth." He continued, "The *contrast* between therapeutic acceptance and sacrificial love might tell us more about love and acceptance than would the quest for analogies between them."[9] We agree with Holifield's call for a historical awareness of how culture has shaped what appear to the practitioner as absolute formulations. We would add to this a call for ministry of the future to rethink its distinctive contribution to the goals of counseling. We would hope that such an awareness becomes a standard for internal, if not external, quality control.

Quantity of Care

Turning next to issues of quantity rather than quality, we may state the issue as "How much service will ministry provide in the future?" Quantity has to do with amount and degree of service, rather than type. The more professional ministry becomes and the more it is divorced from the local church, the more it may tend to operate within time limits and fee-for-service models. These are the boundaries within which professions such as medicine and law function in our society. But is this Christian ministry? Is not Christian ministry more likely to function in a manner resembling Pastor McArthur's taking a disturbed young man into his home to live for a while after his discharge from the hospital—as recounted in the testimony of the Grace Community Church case? Ministry in the future must face the issue of how much love and availability it will offer to those it serves. Although there are definite human limits to ministerial availability, the genius of the unmarried priesthood has been the presumption that ministers go when needed and stay until the need no longer exists. Presumably, nothing is to stand in the way or distract them from that task. How will professional ministers deal with this in the future, and will they be accused of malpractice if they do not meet their clients' expectations in these regards? A less individualistic approach would consider the whole church as ministry, with laity assuming many of the roles that an individual pastor could not.

Some of what has been said to this point has been descriptive; some of it has been prescriptive. That is to say, our predictions about the future of ministry have been based in part on what we think the situation *will* be and in part on what we think the situation *should* be. The descriptive portion of our discussion has been grounded in our understanding of cultural changes and our understanding of the nature of professionalism. The prescriptive portion has been based on our understanding of the biblical revelation and the nature of church ministry as a response to the gospel. All in all, our hope would be that those who intend to be a part of ministry's future would not be swept along by either the tides of culture or the ministerial structures of the past. Ministry in the future demands more than this. It cannot be determined by professional self-protectiveness or by pseudo spirituality or a separatist mentality. Ministry in the future will best be served by an intentionality and a method. To this we now turn.

A Method for Future Ministry

One of the best approaches to ministry in the future is contained in James and Evelyn Whitehead's volume *Method in Ministry: Theological Reflection and Christian Ministry.* Our intent is to review their model briefly and to recommend it as a means of being intentional about ministry.

The Whiteheads begin by defining "method." They quote Lonergan's definition: Method is "a normative pattern of recurrent and related operations yielding cumulative and progressive results." In terms of ministry in the future, it should be guided by "normative and recurrent operations"—meaning a set of repeated procedures for reflection that have been well thought out on the basis of what good ministry *should* include. The outcome of this process should result in "cumulative and progressive results"—meaning that future ministry should meet its goals, have its intended effect.[10]

The goal or effect of ministry needs to be clarified before we consider the method in more detail. Ministerial effectiveness could be conceived as the process of helping persons to understand themselves and their experience from the perspective of Almighty God's purpose, presence, and power, coupled with efforts to help those persons to act on that understanding.

Method, therefore, could be conceived as that intentional and planned set of procedures by which future ministers can assure that their ministry will assist persons in Christian self-understanding and behavior.

The method that the Whiteheads recommend involves three components, which are to be consciously related to each other in dialogical fashion. The components are Christian tradition, the experience of the community of faith, and the resources of culture. These are "three sources of religious relevant information." Ministry in every age is under the constant temptation to weight the pressure of the current situation more heavily than it should. When this is done, ministry becomes reactive rather than responsive. The method that the Whiteheads recommend involves being responsive and reflective by weighting tradition, experience, and culture equally.[11]

The first component of the method, Christian tradition, refers to the guidance that ministry can receive from the Bible and from church history. The Bible represents the truth about who humans are and how life ought to be structured. Church history represents the attempt of faithful ministers who have sought to mediate these truths and to guide persons in their daily response to God. No ministry in the future should be attempted without reference to these sources of the Christian tradition. Many difficulties, both in the present and the future, can be traced to a neglect of this element.

The second component of the method, the experience of the community of faith, refers to the guidance that ministry can receive from the local church. Ministry in the future—whether specialized or not, tent-making or full-time—should be informed by discussion with others in the community of faith. It is here that experience in the present is brought to bear on the nature of ministry. It is important to note that this type of reflection does not occur simply by mail surveys or home visits. Rather, it occurs under the roof of the church where the community is gathered to share and discuss issues. It occurs in the true-to-life dialogue among Christians who are seeking to be honest about their fears and feelings at the same time that they are attempting to respond in faith to their time and place. It is not a pious glossing but a sincere effort to relate the good news to the daily news! The extent to which future ministry ignores this component will be the extent to which it fails.

The third component of the method, the resources of culture, refers to the guidance that ministry can receive from culture. This includes the contributions of scholars to human self-understanding. It also includes analysis of daily problem solving and of the experience of living in a given environment. The Whiteheads note that this type of information can be both positive and negative. While there are resources in the culture which inform both the direction and the form ministry should take, there are, on the other hand, aspects of culture which evidence an almost demonic tendency to influence humans to live as if there were no God. Future ministry must be able to distinguish between negative and positive resources and to resist the temptation toward fadism and technology.

Turning next to the procedure whereby these components of ministry can be related to each other, the Whiteheads suggest a three-step procedure: attending, assertion, and decision. Attending involves intentional attempts to seek out information on a particular ministerial issue from the three components of tradition, experience, and culture. Assertion involves engaging in a process of dialogue, individually or interpersonally, with the information that is gleaned from the attending step. Decision involves self-consciously moving from the ministerial insights emerging from the assertion process to a decision to act in a given manner.

Such a method as the Whiteheads suggest has much value for answering the question "What will be the shape of ministry in the future?" It is our conviction that ministry in the future will have no need to be ashamed, nor need it fear legal action for malpractice, if it follows a process of reflection such as we have outlined. There will always be a risk to ministry—but that is as it should be. Those who are seeking a ministry with guaranteed safety should look elsewhere for their vocations. However, risk and responsibility are two different things. Responsible ministry, that which genuinely and thoughtfully attempts to relate the transcendent to the mundane, will always run the risk of being challenged by those who want nothing to do with the divine, on the one hand, or nothing to do with the human, on the other. This is a risk which is well known.

We suspicion that this lack of balance in ministry is a part of the case involving Grace Community Church. Although we do not mean to condone all that the church did, we do wish to note that it was attempting to understand human problems from a divine perspective. The effort may have been misguided but the effort was there just the same. We should hasten to add that, in terms of cure, the nonreligious sources of care had had no greater success than the church in dealing with the troubled young man.

As Melton and Moore pointed out in their book *The Cult Experience: Responding to the New Religious Pluralism*,[12] there exists too ready a tendency to embrace criticisms of unfamiliar religious activity without realizing that such criticisms often come from those who are basically against a religious interpretation of life of any kind. This tendency may underlie the acceptance of negative reports of the cult experience such as that written by the psychologist Margaret Singer,[13] in which she bemoans the fact that former cult devotees took over a year to return to productive adjustment to society. Her analysis embodies an unexamined affirmation of "society" without any sense that society may need a religious critique. Future ministry should never be content with such a simplistic appraisal.

There will be ministry in the future. The early-twentieth-century predictions that science would take over for religion have not been realized. Religious needs have been found to be perennial, and there will always be a need for ministers. If our insights are correct, ministry in the future will become increasingly specialized and tent-making. This will involve a tendency toward professionalism which will expose ministry to issues of quality and quantity control. An increasingly aware and litigious society will challenge ministry more and more. Malpractice suits will increase. However, ministry in the future need have no fear if it intentionally and self-consciously follows such a method as we have outlined. Although ministry may be challenged, it will not run the risk of being unfaithful to its task if it attends to Christian tradition, seeks counsel from the community, and applies its understandings to culture. If it does not adopt such a method, it may never be challenged in a court of law but it will have failed at a much deeper and more serious level.

Appendix:
Codes of Professional Ethics

I. American Association for Marriage and Family Therapy
Ethical Principles for Family Therapists

1. Responsibility to Clients

Family therapists are dedicated to advancing the welfare of families and individuals, including respecting the rights of those persons seeking their assistance, and making reasonable efforts to ensure that their services are used appropriately.

1.1 Family therapists do not discriminate against or refuse professional service to anyone on the basis of race, sex, religion, or national origin.

1.2 Family therapists do not use their professional relationship to further personal, religious, political, or business interests. Sexual intimacy with clients is unethical.

1.3 Family therapists continue a therapeutic relationship only so long as it is reasonably clear that clients are benefiting from the relationship.

1.4 Family therapists make financial arrangements with clients that are consistent with normal and accepted professional practices and that are reasonably understandable to clients.

Adopted September 1982. Reprinted with permission.

1.5 Family therapists respect the rights of clients to make decisions consistent with their age and other relevant conditions, while retaining responsibility for assessing the situation according to sound professional judgment and sharing such judgment with the clients. Family therapists clearly advise a client that a decision on marital status is the responsibility of the client.

1.6 Family therapists accept the responsibility for providing services to clients in accordance with AAMFT standards for delivery of family therapy services.

2. Competence

Family therapists are dedicated to maintaining high standards of competence, recognizing appropriate limitations to their competence and services and using consultation from other professionals.

2.1 Family therapists seek appropriate professional assistance for personal problems or conflicts that are likely to impair their work performance.

2.2 Family therapists, as teachers, are dedicated to maintaining high standards of scholarship and presenting information that is scholarly, up-to-date, and accurate.

2.3 Family therapists do not attempt to diagnose, treat, or advise on problems outside the recognized boundaries of their competence.

3. Integrity

Family therapists are honest in dealing with clients, students, trainees, colleagues, and the public, seeking to eliminate incompetence or dishonesty from the work or representations of family therapists.

3.1 Family therapists do not claim, either directly or by implication, professional qualifications exceeding those actually attained, including the presentation of degrees from nonaccredited institutions or programs.

3.2 Family therapists do not use false or misleading advertising or use advertising that in any way violates the AAMFT's "Standards on Public Information and Advertising." Also, they abide by the AAMFT regulations regarding the use of the AAMFT logo.

3.3 Family therapists accept the responsibility to correct wherever possible misleading and inaccurate information and representations made by others concerning the family therapist's qualifications, services, or products.

3.4 Family therapists have the obligation to make certain that the qualifications of persons in their employ are appropriate to the services provided and are appropriately represented.

3.5 Family therapists neither offer nor accept payment for referrals.

3.6 Family therapists accept the responsibility for making informed corrective efforts with other family therapists who are violating ethical principles or for bringing the violations to the attention of the Ethics Committee or other appropriate authority. Proper attention to confidentiality shall be given in such efforts.

3.7 Family therapists do not engage in sexual harassment in their working relationships with clients, students, trainees, or colleagues

3.8 Family therapists do not use their relationships with students or trainees to further their own personal, religious, political, or business interests. Sexual intimacy with students or trainees is unethical.

3.9 Family therapists use their membership in AAMFT only in connection with their clinical and professional activities.

4. Confidentiality

Family therapists respect both the law and the rights of clients and safeguard client confidences as permitted by law.

4.1 Family therapists use clinical materials in teaching, writing, and public presentations only when permission has been obtained or when appropriate steps have been taken to protect client identity.

4.2 Family therapists store or dispose of client records in ways that enhance safety and confidentiality.

4.3 Family therapists communicate information about clients to others only after obtaining appropriate client consent, unless there is a clear and immediate danger to an individual or to society, and then only to the concerned individual and appropriate family members, professional workers, or public authorities.

5. Professional Responsibility

Family therapists respect the rights and responsibilities of professional colleagues and, as employees of organizations, remain accountable as individuals to the ethical principles of their profession.

5.1 Family therapists assign publication credit to those who have contributed to a publication in proportion to their contributions and in accordance with customary professional publication practices.

5.2 Family therapists who are the authors of books or other materials that are published or distributed should cite appropriately persons to whom credit for original ideas is due.

5.3 Family therapists who are the authors of books or other materials published or distributed by an organization take reasonable precautions to ensure that the organization promotes and advertises the materials accurately and factually.

6. Professional Development

Family therapists seek to continue their professional development and strive to make pertinent knowledge available to clients, students, trainees, colleagues, and the public.

6.1 Family therapists seek to remain abreast of new developments in family therapy knowledge and practice through both formal educational activities and informal learning experiences.

6.2 Family therapists who supervise or employ trainees, family therapists, or other professionals assume a reasonable obligation to encourage and enhance the professional development of those persons.

6.3 Family therapists who provide supervision assume responsibility for defining the relationships as "supervisor-supervisee" and for clearly defining and separating supervisory and therapeutic roles and relationships.

7. Research Responsibility

Family therapists recognize that, while research is essential to the advancement of knowledge, all investigations must be conducted with full respect for the rights and dignity of participants and with full concern for their welfare.

7.1 Family therapists, as researchers, strive to be adequately informed of relevant laws and other regulations regarding the conduct of research with human participants and to abide by those laws and regulations.

7.2 Family therapists, as researchers, assume responsibility for ensuring that their research is conducted in an ethical manner.

8. Social Responsibility

Family therapists acknowledge a responsibility to participate in activities that contribute to a better community and society, including devoting a portion of their professional activity to services for which there is little or no financial return.

8.1 Family therapists are concerned with developing laws and legal regulations pertaining to family therapy that serve the public interest and with altering such laws and regulations that are not in the public interest.

8.2 Family therapists affirm that professional services involve both practitioner and client and seek to encourage public participation in the designing and delivery of services and in the regulation of practitioners.

II. American Association of Pastoral Counselors Code of Ethics

I. General

Pastoral counselors are committed to a belief in God and in the dignity and worth of each individual. They accept and maintain in their own personal lives the highest ethical standards, but do not judge others by these standards.

The maintenance of high standards of professional competence is a responsibility shared by all pastoral counselors in the interests of the public, the religious community, and the profession. The pastoral counselor works toward the improvement and refinement of counseling through the establishment of ethical standards in pastoral counseling generally and especially at all pastoral counseling centers.

Pastoral counselors are accountable for their total ministry whatever its setting. This accountability is expressed in relationship to clients, colleagues, and the faith community, and in the acceptance of, and practice based upon, this Code of Ethics of the Association.

In the practice of the profession, pastoral counselors show sensible regard for moral, social, and religious standards, realizing that any violation on their part may be damaging to their clients, students, and colleagues and to their profession.

II. Professional Practices

In all professional matters pastoral counselors maintain practices that protect the public and advance the profession.

A. Pastoral counselors accurately represent their professional qualifications and their affiliation with any institution, organization, or individual. Pastoral counselors are responsible for correcting any misrepresentation of their professional qualifications or affiliations.

B. Pastoral counselors use their knowledge or professional association for the benefit of the people they serve and not to secure unfair personal advantage, consistent with the standards and purposes of the Association.

C. Members of the Association clearly represent their level of membership and limit their practice at their respective level.

Adopted May 2, 1981. Reprinted with permission.

D. Announcements of pastoral counseling services are dignified, accurate, and objective, descriptive but devoid of all claims or evaluation.

E. Brochures that promote the services of a pastoral counseling center describe them with accuracy and dignity. They may be sent to professional persons, religious institutions, and other agencies, but to prospective individual clients only in response to inquiries.

F. Financial arrangements are always discussed at the start and handled in a businesslike manner. Pastoral counselors stand ready to render service to individuals and communities in crisis, without regard to financial remuneration, when necessary.

G. Pastoral counselors neither receive nor pay a commission for referral of a client.

H. Records on clients are stored in a place assuring security and confidentiality.

I. Pastoral counselors avoid disparagement of a colleague or other professional person to a client.

III. Client Relationship and Confidentiality
Pastoral counselors respect the integrity and protect the welfare of persons or groups with whom they are working, and have an obligation to safeguard information about them that has been obtained in the course of the counseling process.

A. It is the duty of pastoral counselors, during the counseling process, to maintain the relationship with the client on a professional basis.

B. Pastoral counselors do not make unrealistic promises regarding the counseling process or its outcome.

C. Pastoral counselors recognize that the religious convictions of a client have powerful emotional and volitional significance and therefore are approached with care and sensitivity. They recognize that their influence may be considerable and therefore avoid any possible imposition of their own theology on clients.

D. Pastoral counselors do not engage in sexual misconduct with their clients.

E. Except by written permission, all communications from clients are treated with professional confidence. When clients are referred to in a publication, their identity is thoroughly disguised and the report shall so state.

F. Ethical concern for the integrity and welfare of the person or group applies to supervisory and training relationships. These relationships are maintained on a professional and confidential basis. Personal therapy will not be provided by one's current supervisor or administrator.

IV. Church Relationship

Pastoral counselors maintain vital association with the faith group in which they have ecclesiastical standing. They work for the improvement and growth of pastoral counseling throughout the religious community. They communicate to their own faith group and the broader religious community the implications for the life of their community of their experience in pastoral counseling. When members of this Association are removed from the ecclesiastical roster of their sponsoring faith group, they are to report it to the Committee of Professional Concerns, for review of their membership.

V. Interprofessional Relationships

Pastoral counselors relate to and cooperate with other professional persons in their community.

A. Pastoral counselors maintain interprofessional relationships, recognizing the importance of developing such relationships for the purposes of clinical consultations and referrals.

B. Pastoral counselors are sensitive to the total health needs of the clients they serve. To this end, they have access to appropriate health care professionals.

C. The affiliation of members with professional and interprofessional groups and organizations in the community is encouraged.

D. Pastoral counselors who offer specialized counseling services to persons currently receiving counseling or therapy from another professional person do so only with prior knowledge by the professional involved. Soliciting such clients is unethical practice.

VI. Professional Development

Pastoral counselors continue postgraduate education and professional growth in many ways, including active participation in the meetings and affairs of the Association. Whenever appropriate, they join with other pastoral counselors and with representatives of other helping professions to promote mutual professional growth.

VII. Publications and Communications

Pastoral counselors distinguish and differentiate their private opinions from those of their denomination or profession in publicity, public pronouncements, or publications.

A. Pastoral counselors communicate the relationship of religion and health and the nature of the healing ministry.

B. Modesty, scientific caution, and due regard for the limits of present knowledge characterize all statements and publications of pastoral counselors who supply information to the public, either directly or indirectly. Exaggeration, sensationalism, superficiality, and other kinds of misrepresentation are unethical.

C. Pastoral counselors do not make it appear, directly or indirectly, that they speak for the Association or represent its official position, except as authorized by the Board of Governors.

VIII. Unethical Conduct

When pastoral counselors are accepted for membership in the Association, they bind themselves to accept the judgment of other members as to standards of professional ethics, subject to the safeguards provided as follows. Acceptance of membership involves explicit agreement to abide by the acts of discipline herein set forth.

Members of this Association are committed to maintain high standards of ethical practice. To this end members consult with their colleagues on the Regional Ethics Committee whenever ethical questions arise, the answers to which do not appear to be clear to them. Members who appear to violate the foregoing Code of Ethics should be cautioned through friendly remonstrance. That failing, formal complaint may be made in accordance with the following procedures:

A. Complaint of unethical practice is made in writing to the Regional Ethics Committee. A copy of the complaint is furnished simultaneously to the person or persons against whom it is directed.

B. The first action of the Regional Ethics Committee is to approach those involved in pastoral concern, seeking a collegial resolution. If the Committee decides the complaint warrants investigation, it may elect from a variety of investigative endeavors including the possibility of one or more local visits.

C. Members have full access and full freedom and right to respond to all complaints and evidence cited against them. They always have the right and option of advisement by counsel at their own expense but at no time to be represented by counsel in these proceedings.

D. Actions taken by the Regional Ethics Committee may include:
   1. Advice that the complaint is unfounded; admonishment, reprimand, or probation.
   2. Recommendation to the National Ethics Committee of suspension or dismissal from membership.

E. Any recommendation for suspension or dismissal with all supporting information and full reports of the Regional Committee's investigation are sent to the National Ethics Committee for Action. In the event of dismissal, members at once surrender their membership certificate to the Ethics Committee for transmission to the National Office.

F. 1. Members or complainants have the right to request review of actions taken by the Regional Ethics Committee as outlined in VIII D 1. above. The request must be made in writing within 30 days, accompanied by appropriate documentation. All supporting information and full reports of the Regional Committee's investigation are sent to the National Committee.
   2. Final appeal of the National Ethics Committee action to suspend or dismiss from membership is to the Board of Governors, following the same procedure.

G. Should a member of this Association be removed by either faith group or another professional group for unethical conduct, the Regional Ethics Committee investigates the matter and acts in the manner provided above.

H. The procedure for reinstatement is the same as for new membership. When an application for reinstatement is received, the Membership Committee consults with the Ethics Committee which had recommended dismissal.

III. American Psychological Association Ethical Principles of Psychologists

Preamble

Psychologists respect the dignity and worth of the individual and strive for the preservation and protection of fundamental human rights. They are committed to increasing knowledge of human behavior and of people's understanding of themselves and others and to the utilization of such knowledge for the promotion of human welfare. While pursuing these objectives, they make every effort to protect the welfare of those who seek their services and of research participants that may be the object of study. They use their skills only for purposes consistent with these values and do not knowingly permit their misuse by others. While demanding for themselves freedom of inquiry and communication, psychologists accept the responsibility this freedom requires: competence, objectivity in the application of skills, and concern for the best interests of clients, colleagues, students, research participants, and society. In the pursuit of these ideals, psychologists subscribe to the following principles:

1. Responsibility

In providing services, psychologists maintain the highest standards of their profession. They accept responsibility for the consequences of their acts and make every effort to ensure that their services are used appropriately. . . .

2. Competence

The maintenance of high standards of competence is a responsibility shared by all psychologists in the interest of the public and the profession as a whole. Psychologists recognize the boundaries of their competence and the limitations of their techniques. They only provide services and only use techniques for which they are qualified by training and experience. In those areas in which recognized standards do not yet exist, psychologists take whatever precautions are necessary to protect the welfare of their clients. They maintain knowledge of current scientific and professional information related to the services they render. . . .

3. Moral and Legal Standards

Psychologists' moral and ethical standards of behavior are a personal matter to the same degree as they are for any other citizen, except as these may compromise the fulfillment of their professional responsibilities or reduce the public trust in psychology and psychologists. Regarding their own behavior, psychologists are sensitive to prevailing community standards and to the possible impact that conformity to or deviation from these standards may have upon the quality of their performance as psychologists. Psychologists are also aware of the possible impact of their public behavior upon the ability of colleagues to perform their professional duties. . . .

4. Public Statements

Public statements, announcements of services, advertising, and promotional activities of psychologists serve the purpose of helping the public make informed judgments and choices. Psychologists represent accurately and objectively their professional qualifications, affiliations, and functions, as well as those of the institutions or organizations with which they or the statements may be associated. In public statements providing psychological information or professional opinions or providing information about the availability of psychological products, publications, and services, psychologists base their statements on scientifically acceptable psychological findings and techniques with full recognition of the limits and uncertainties of such evidence. . . .

5. Confidentiality

Psychologists have a primary obligation to respect the confidentiality of information obtained from persons in the course of their work as psychologists. They reveal such information to others only with the consent of the person or the person's legal representative, except in those unusual circumstances in which not to do so would result in clear danger to the person or to others. Where appropriate, psychologists inform their clients of the legal limits of confidentiality. . . .

6. Welfare of the Consumer

Psychologists respect the integrity and protect the welfare of the people and groups with whom they work. When conflicts of interest arise between clients and psychologists' employing institutions, psychologists clarify the nature and direction of their loyalties and responsibilities and keep all parties informed of their commitments. Psychologists fully inform consumers as to the purpose and nature of an evaluative, treatment, educational, or training procedure, and they freely acknowledge that clients, students, or participants in research have freedom of choice with regard to participation. . . .

7. Professional Relationships

Psychologists act with due regard for the needs, special competencies, and obligations of their colleagues in psychology and other professions. They respect the prerogatives and obligations of the institutions or organizations with which these other colleagues are associated. . . .

8. Assessment Techniques

In the development, publication, and utilization of psychological assessment techniques, psychologists make every effort to promote the welfare and best interests of the client. They guard against the misuse of assessment results. They respect the client's right to know the results, the interpretations made, and the bases for their conclusions and recommendations. Psychologists make every effort to maintain the security of tests and other assessment techniques within limits of legal mandates. They strive to ensure the appropriate use of assessment techniques by others. . . .

9. Research with Human Participants

The decision to undertake research rests upon a considered judgment by the individual psychologist about how best to contribute to psychological science and human welfare. Having made the decision to conduct research, the psychologist considers alternative directions in which research energies and resources might be invested. On the basis of this consideration, the psychologist carries out the investigation with respect and concern for the dignity and welfare of the people who participate and with cognizance of federal and state regulations and professional standards governing the conduct of research with human participants. . . .

10. Care and Use of Animals

An investigator of animal behavior strives to advance understanding of basic behavioral principles and/or to contribute to the improvement of human health and welfare. In seeking these ends, the investigator ensures the welfare of animals and treats them humanely. Laws and regulations notwithstanding, an animal's immediate protection depends upon the scientist's own conscience. . . .

IV. Christian Association for Psychological Studies Proposed Code of Ethics

Applicability of the Code

This Code of Ethics (hereinafter referred to as the "Code") is applicable to all current, dues-paid Members and Associate Members of the Christian Association for Psychological Studies (CAPS). While CAPS is not a licensing or accrediting agency, it does desire that members who provide mental health, pastoral or other personal services do so with the highest possible level of Christian and service or ministry ethics, whether professional, layperson or student. Further, even though CAPS is not a licensing or accrediting agency, it does have the authority to set and monitor qualifications for membership in good standing. Thus, the Board of Directors urges each member to consider carefully and prayerfully the Code and to adopt it personally.

Biblical Foundation

Note: Each of the biblical building blocks of the foundation that follows has one or more references. The references are not exhaustive, nor are they meant to be convenient "proof-texting." Rather, the Scriptures cited are meant to be representative of the many biblical references that build the foundation of this Code. The complete foundation is the total message of the Gospel of Jesus Christ. Also, it is recognized that each believer in Christ has the capacity—even the privilege and duty—to explore the depths of God's Word and discover personal guidance for daily living. This Code could not hope to explore all the richness of the Bible as it relates to ethical conduct.

Biblical "Building Blocks" of the Foundation

Conflicts, difficulties, power struggles, trials and tribulations are normal and to be expected, whether one is a Christian or not (John 16:33; Psalm 37:7, Romans 2:9).

We are to grow and mature through the conflicts, problems, trials and tribulations, and discipline that we experience (James 1:2-4; I Thessalonians 5:18).

We are to support and encourage each other (John 15:17; Ephesians 4:32; John 13:35).

We are to admonish and, if necessary, discipline each other, especially those Christians in positions of leadership and trust. However, such discipline is to be constructive

Approved by the Board of the Western Region, April 1985. Reprinted by permission.

rather than judgmental, done in love, and with caution about our own shortcomings (Matthew 18:15-17; I Corinthians 5: 11-13; Galatians 6:1).

We are to demonstrate the lordship of Christ in our lives by servant-like leadership, a sense of community, and a life style that reflects the will of God (Matthew 20:25-28; John 12:26; I Peter 4:8-11; Colossians 3:12-17).

We are to reach out to others in love and concern (Matthew 25:31-40; Hebrews 13:16; II Corinthians 1:3-7).

Basic Criteria and Principles

1. The Code includes a broad range of morality, yet it is specific enough in certain areas to offer guidance for ethical conduct in a variety of situations. It is intended to be universal without being platitudinous. On the other hand, it aims to be functional without being legalistic.

2. The Code calls for commitment to a distinctively Christian code of ethical behavior in our helping professions. Yet it recognizes that ethical behavior is certainly not the hallmark only of Christians. Thus there is no implication of judging persons of different faiths or value systems.

3. The Code is not a credo or doctrinal statement of CAPS. Article II of the CAPS Constitution and By-Laws contains the basis for our association:
   The basis of this organization is belief in: God, the Father, who creates and sustains us; Jesus Christ, the Son, who redeems and rules us; and the Holy Spirit, who guides us personally and professionally, through God's inspired Word, the Bible, our infallible guide of faith and conduct, and through the communion of Christians.

4. The Code is not a position paper on major social issues. While CAPS has genuine interest in social issues, it has traditionally encouraged members to become involved personally, as led by God, rather than as prescribed by CAPS. Also, CAPS has traditionally encouraged the free exchange of ideas among members, rather than defining "truth" or a partisan viewpoint for its members.

5. All humans are created in the image of God. We are holistic in our being and thus most descriptions of our parts, such as mind, body, soul, spirit, personality, or whatever, are primarily to make it easier to discuss and evaluate our

nature. Much of being created in the image of God is still a mystery to us. However, it does mean that we and those persons we serve have basic dignity and worth, along with basic human rights and essential human responsibilities. Also, we are to glorify God in worship, service, and stewardship.

6. The family is the basic unit of our culture; it merits honor, encouragement, and protection. In addition, "family" to the Christian includes our "neighbor" (Luke 10:29-37). Thus, our "circle of love" embraces God, neighbor, and self (Luke 10:27). Not only that, we are to love our enemies (Matthew 5:43). Also, our influence, our activities in the helping professions, are to be "salt and light" in this world (Matthew 5:13, 14).

7. Scientific and humanistic activities in the helping professions are good, even excellent, but not good enough. While love without professional standards can become mere sentimentality, scientific observations and professional standards without love and Godly ethics can become mere clinical experiments. Thus, the Christian is called to maximize helping others by integrating the distinctives of Christian commitment—including prayer—with professional education, training, and, if appropriate, licensing.

8. The world as we know it is a temporal place of human existence with the ever-present contrasts or polarities such as good and evil, order and disorder, joy and sorrow, generosity and selfishness, love and apathy, abundance and scarcity. Further, we do not necessarily know the reasons for any particular situation, event, or relationship.

9. Exploiting or manipulating another person for our own or yet another's pleasure or aggrandizement is unethical and sinful.

10. Pretending to have expertise beyond our abilities or practicing beyond the scope of our licensure is unethical, very likely illegal, and does not value the person who needs help, nor does it glorify God.

11. Attempting to do for others what they are able and responsible to do for themselves, especially those persons who are seeking counsel, tends to create dependency and is thus unethical.

12. Some persons—such as children—are more dependent than others and thus merit a greater degree of protection from persons who would thoughtlessly or selfishly take advantage of or manipulate them.

13. Each of us, whether helper or the person being helped, is a fallible human being who has limits that are universal in human nature yet unique in magnitude and proportion within each individual.

14. The helping professions are both art and science, with much to be learned. Also, each of us who serves, whether as professional or layperson, needs to be competent enough in what we do and of sufficient personal stability and integrity that what we do promotes healing rather than disorder and harm.

Note: In an effort to avoid awkward and lengthy descriptions of persons we serve, the somewhat neutral word "client" is used. According to the perspective of members, words such as "peer," "parishioner," "communicant," "patient," "help-ee," "counselee," or even "prisoner" may be used.

Also, the word "service" or "serving" is used frequently in the Code to describe what we do. Again, according to the perspective of members, words such as "helping ministries," "helping professions," "counseling," "ministering," or "pastoring," for example, may be substituted. Admittedly, no word is neutral, since language shapes (and reflects) our reality. Thus the word "service" or its derivatives is meant to reflect Christ's statement that he came to serve, rather than to be served.

1. Personal Commitment as a Christian

1.1 I agree with the basis of CAPS, as quoted earlier in this Code, stated in the Constitution and By-Laws.

1.2 I commit my service, whether as professional or layperson, to God as a special calling.

1.3 I pledge to integrate all that I do in service with Christian values, principles, and guidelines.

1.4 I commit myself to Christ as Lord as well as Savior. Thus, direction and wisdom from God will be sought, while accepting responsibility for my own actions and statements.

1.5 I view my body as the temple of the Holy Spirit and will treat it lovingly and respectfully. Balance in my priorities will be prayerfully sought.

2. *Loving Concern for Clients*

2.1 Clients will be accepted regardless of race, religion, gender, income, education, ethnic background, value system, etc., unless such a factor would interfere appreciably with my ability to be of service.

2.2 I value human life, the sanctity of personhood, personal freedom, and responsibility, and the privilege of free choice in matters of belief and action.

2.3 I will avoid exploiting or manipulating any client to satisfy my own needs.

2.4 I will abstain from undue invasion of privacy.

2.5 I will take appropriate actions to help, even protect, those persons who are relatively dependent on other persons for their survival and well-being.

2.6 Sexual intimacy with any client will be scrupulously avoided.

3. *Confidentiality*

3.1 I will demonstrate utmost respect for the confidentiality of the client and other persons in the helping relationship.

3.2 The limits of confidentiality, such as those based on civil laws, regulations, and judicial precedent, will be explained to the client.

3.3 I will carefully protect the identity of clients and their problems. Thus I will avoid divulging information about clients, whether privately or publicly, unless I have informed consent of the client, given by express written permission, and the release of such information would be appropriate to the situation.

3.4 All records of counseling will be handled in a way that protects the clients and the nature of their problems from disclosure.

4. Competency in Services Provided

4.1 I pledge to be well-trained and competent in providing services.

4.2 I will refrain from implying that I have qualifications, experiences, and capabilities which are in fact lacking.

4.3 I will comply with applicable state and local laws and regulations regarding the helping professions.

4.4 I will avoid using any legal exemptions from counseling competency afforded in certain states to churches and other nonprofit organizations as a means of providing services that are beyond my training and expertise.

4.5 I will diligently pursue additional education, experience, professional consultation, and spiritual growth in order to improve my effectiveness in serving persons in need.

5. My Human Limitations

5.1 I will do my best to be aware of my human limitations and biases and openly admit that I do not have scientific objectivity or spiritual maturity, insofar as my subjective viewpoint will permit.

5.2 I will avoid fostering any misconception a client could have that I am omnipotent or that I have all the answers.

5.3 I will refer clients whom I am not capable of counseling, whether by lack of available time or expertise or even because of subjective personal reasons. The referral will be done compassionately, clearly, and completely, insofar as feasible.

5.4 I will resist efforts of any clients or colleagues to place demands for services on me that exceed my qualifications and/or the time available to minister, or that would impose unduly on my relationship with my own family.

6. Advertising and Promotional Activities

6.1 I will advertise or promote my services by Christian and professional standards, rather than commercial standards.

6.2 Personal aggrandizement will be omitted from advertising and promotional activities.

7. Research

7.1 Any research conducted will be done openly and will not jeopardize the welfare of any persons who are research, i.e., test, subjects. Further, clients will not be used as publicly identifiable test subjects.

8. Unethical Conduct, Confrontation, and Malpractice

8.1 If I have sufficient reason to believe a Christian colleague in CAPS has been practicing or ministering in a way that is probably damaging to the client or the helping ministries, I will confront that person. The principles and procedures specified in Matthew 18:15–17 will be followed in confronting the person who appears to be behaving unethically. In addition, the more stringent actions against pastors specified in I Timothy 5:19–20 will be considered, if relevant.

8.2 In addition to the confrontation procedures based on scriptural guidance, civil law will be followed if relevant or applicable.

8.3 If the CAPS Board becomes aware that a member has been accused of unethical conduct, the Ethics Committee (either standing or ad hoc) will investigate the situation and recommend ethical discipline, including expulsion from membership, if appropriate.

8.3.1 If a person has been expelled from membership for unethical conduct, the Ethics Committee will maintain loving and concerned liaison with the person and others involved, as appropriate, and will attempt to bring about actions for repentance, forgiveness, and restoration into the membership.

8.4 The Ethics Committee will also provide consultation to CAPS as an organization and to individual members who may be confronting ethical dilemmas and want some guidance.

8.4.1 Since ethical concerns may be complex and have legal implications, the consultation provided will be primarily in helping think through a situation, without assuming responsibility for the case.

8.5 The value of malpractice insurance will be carefully considered, especially if a lawsuit—whether justified or not—would possibly drain financial resources of the ministry organization with which I am associated, or of my family.

9 General Prudential Rule

9.1 Recognizing that no code of ethics is complete, I will make day-to-day decisions based on the criteria and principles stated at the beginning of this Code. Even more important, I will do my best to serve and to live in a way that is congruent with the stated basic principles of this Code and with my faith as a Christian.

Notes

1. Malpractice in the Ministry/Needham

1. For a discussion of three reasons why attorney Richard Hammar believes clergy malpractice suits will not be successful, see pp. 73–75 of his *Pastor, Church, and Law* (Gospel Publishing House, 1983).

2. John Dart, "Clergy Malpractice Suit Dismissed," *The Christian Century,* May 29, 1985, p. 548.

3. "California Judge Dismisses Nation's First 'Clergy Malpractice' Suit," *Christianity Today,* June 14, 1985, p. 49.

4. Laurence P. Feldman, *Consumer Protection: Problems and Prospects,* 2nd ed. (West Publishing Co., 1980), p. 2.

5. Ibid., pp. 12–18.

6. Dennis M. Campbell, *Doctors, Lawyers, Ministers: Christian Ethics in Professional Practice* (Abingdon Press, 1982), p. 37.

7. Henry Campbell Black, *Black's Law Dictionary: Definitions of the Terms and Phrases of American and English Jurisprudence, Ancient and Modern,* 4th ed., rev. (West Publishing Co., 1968), p. 1111.

8. "Alarm Over Malpractice," *Time,* January 28, 1985, p. 75.

9. Nicholas A. Cummings and Suzanne B. Sobel, "Malpractice Insurance; Update on Sex Claims," *Psychotherapy,* vol. 22, no. 2 (1985), p. 187.

10. Letter from Dr. Nicholas A. Cummings, Chair, American Psychological Association Insurance Trust, December 17, 1984.

11. Cummings and Sobel, p. 186.

12. Edward Farley, "Theology and Practice Outside the Clerical Paradigm," ch. 1 in *Practical Theology,* ed. by Don S. Browning (Harper & Row, 1983), p. 23.

13. Ibid., p. 29.

14. Don S. Browning, *The Moral Context of Pastoral Care* (Westminster Press, 1976), p. 118.

15. Paul W. Pruyser, *The Minister as Diagnostician: Personal Problems in Pastoral Perspective* (Westminster Press, 1976).

16. See Samuel Southard, *Pastoral Authority in Personal Relationships* (Abingdon Press, 1969), pp. 89, 90; Thomas C. Oden, *Contemporary Theology and Psychotherapy* (Westminster Press, 1967).

17. Browning, Introduction to *Practical Theology*, p. 14.

18. Browning, *Moral Context*, pp. 27–31.

19. Ibid., p. 11.

20. William S. Sahakian, *History and Systems of Psychology* (John Wiley & Sons/Halsted Press, 1975), pp. 286–290.

21. Don S. Browning, *Pluralism and Personality: William James and Some Contemporary Cultures of Psychology* (Associated University Press, 1980), p. 212.

22. *Time*, September 2, 1985, p. 49.

23. John F. Cleary, "Clergy Malpractice: The Insurance Carrier's Perspective," unpublished paper, 1985, p. 7.

24. *Carrieri v. Bush, Pacific Reporter* 2d, vol. 419, p. 132 (1966).

25. Ibid.

26. Ibid., p. 5.

27. *Nally v. Grace Community Church of the Valley* (1984), *California Appellate Reports* 3d, vol. 157, p. 939.

28. "Clergy Malpractice Case Dismissal," *California State Psychological Association Newsletter*, vol. 20, no. 5 (July/August 1985), p. 1.

29. Ibid.

30. Cleary, op. cit. note 23, p. 9.

31. Ibid., p. 8.

32. *Smotrich v. Hillel Silverman and Sinai Temple*, No. C353–230 (Los Angeles Superior Court, filed June 29, 1984).

33. Ibid.

34. *Quinn v. Collinsville Church of Christ*, No. CT–81–929 (Oklahoma District Court, 1984), appeal pending (Oklahoma Superior Court, 1985).

35. *Brown v. Fairview Church of Christ*, No. 427764 (County of Orange Superior Court, filed April 20, 1984).

36. *Kelly v. Christian Community Church*, No. 545117 (County of Santa Clara Superior Court, filed June 4, 1985).

37. Ibid., Motion for Summary Judgment (August 1, 1985).

38. Ibid., Motion for Summary Judgment denied September 11, 1985.

39. *Edwards v. St. Stephen's Episcopal Church*, No. 844020 (San Francisco County Superior Court, filed August 5, 1985).

2. What the Law Says

Ramifications of a New Theory/Ericsson

1. William L. Prosser, *Handbook of the Law of Torts,* 3rd ed. (West Publishing Co., 1964), p. 14.
2. *Liberty,* March–April 1980, pp. 15–17.
3. *Nally v. Grace Community Church of the Valley,* No. NCC-18668-B (Los Angeles County Superior Court, California, filed March 31, 1980). On October 2, 1981, summary judgment was granted as to all defendants on all counts by Judge Thomas J. Murphy, Superior Court of Los Angeles County, in Burbank, California. In addition, the court ordered the plaintiffs to reimburse the defendants for their costs.
4. *Sacramento Union,* May 6, 1980, p. A7. Subsequent research has shown that it appears to be the first such case anywhere.
5. These are: (1) a duty or obligation, recognized by the law, requiring the actor to conform to a certain standard of conduct for the protection of others against unreasonable risks and (2) a failure on his part to conform to the standard required (these two elements go to make up what the courts usually have called negligence, but the term quite frequently is applied to the second alone; thus it may be said that the defendant was negligent but is not liable because he was under no duty to the plaintiff not to be); (3) a reasonably close causal connection between the conduct and the resulting injury (this is what is commonly known as "legal cause" or "proximate cause"; and (4) actual loss or damage resulting to the interests of another (Prosser, op. cit., p. 146).
6. Thomas S. Szasz, "The Theology of Therapy: The Breach of the First Amendment Through the Medicalization of Morals," *New York University Review of Law and Social Change,* vol. 5, pp. 127, 133–135 (1975) (emphasis added).
7. Karl Menninger, *Whatever Became of Sin?* (Hawthorn Books, 1972).
8. O. Hobart Mowrer, *The Crisis in Psychiatry and Religion* (D. Van Nostrand Co., 1961), p. 60.
9. Mowrer, "Sin, the Lesser of Two Evils," *American Psychologist,* vol. 15 (1960), p. 301.
10. Ibid., p. 304 (emphasis added).
11. Paul C. Vitz, *Psychology as Religion: The Cult of Self-Worship* (Wm. B. Eerdmans Publishing Co., 1977).
12. Ibid., p. 10.
13. Ibid.
14. For example, compare the standards of care set out in *California Jury Instructions—Civil: Book of Approved Jury Instructions* (6th rev. ed., 1977): 6.00, "Duty of Physician and Surgeon"; 6.01, "Duty of Specialist"; 6.25, "Duty of a Nurse," etc.
15. Ibid.
16. Harvey M. Weinstein and Michael L. Russell, "Competency-

Based Psychiatric Education," *American Journal of Psychiatry*, vol. 133 (August 1976), p. 935.

17. Jay E. Adams, *Competent to Counsel* (Presbyterian & Reformed Publishing Co., 1970), ch. 3. See also John 14:16–17.

18. Research has failed to disclose a single case where the content of the counsel given by a psychiatrist or a psychologist was the issue. There have been a few cases where hospitals, jails, and psychiatrists have been held liable for negligence in the care granted a patient or prisoner in their custody. *Visticia v. Presbyterian Hospital and Medical Center*, California Reports 2d, vol. 67, p. 465; Pacific Reporter 2d, vol. 432, p. 193; West's California Reporter, vol. 62, p. 577 (1967): plaintiff's decedent admitted to psychiatric ward of hospital under the care of a psychiatrist jumps from window, killing self; see also *Meier v. Ross General Hospital*, California Reports 2d, vol. 69, p. 420; Pacific Reporter 2d, vol. 445, p. 519; California Reporter, vol. 71, page 903 (1968).

19. J. W. Whitehead and J. Conlan, "The Establishment of the Religion of Secular Humanism and Its First Amendment Implications" *Texas Tech Law Review*, vol. 10, no. 1, p. 35 (1978).

20. See, e.g., California Evidence Code Sections 1030–1034 (West, 1966).

21. California Reports 3d, vol. 2, p. 415; Pacific Reporter 2d, vol. 467, p. 557; West's California Reporter, vol. 85, p. 829 (1970).

22. Pacific Reporter 2d, vol. 467, p. 565; West's California Reporter, vol. 85, p. 837 (emphasis added; citations omitted).

23. *Valladao v. Firemen's Fund Indemnity Co.*, California Reports 2d, vol. 13, pp. 322, 328–329; Pacific Reporter 2d, vol. 89, pp. 643, 646 (1939).

24. See, e.g., note 14, 6.04, "Duty to Refer to Specialist."

25. One might also question the wisdom of placing pastors, priests, rabbis, and other spiritual counselors under a legal duty to refer any of their flock to the "professionals," since the unfortunate fact is that the highest rate of suicide is found among physicians. Moreover, the suicide rate is significantly higher among psychiatrists than among those of any of the other sixteen specialty groups listed by the American Medical Association as part of the medical profession. *Bulletin of Suicidology*, vol. 5 (December 1968), cited by Adams in *Competent to Counsel*, p. 21. In fact, no less than seven of Freud's early disciples died by suicide. Perr, "Suicide Responsibility of Hospital and Psychiatrist," *Cleveland Maritime Law Review*, vol. 9, pp. 427, 433 (1960).

26. California Business and Professions Code, section 2146 (West, 1974).

27. Ibid., section 4508.

28. Ibid., section 17800.1.

29. 322 U.S., p. 78 (1944).

30. Ibid., p. 81.

31. Ibid., p. 82.
32. Ibid., p. 83.
33. Ibid., pp. 86–87 (citations omitted).
34. Ibid., p. 93.
35. Ibid.
36. Ibid.
37. Ibid.
38. Ibid., p. 94.
39. Ibid., pp. 94–95.
40. See notes 52ff. and accompanying text.
41. Compare *Davis v. Veason*, 133 U.S., pp. 333, 342 (1890), and *Cantwell v. Connecticut*, 310 U.S., p. 296 (1940), with *United States v. Seeger*, 380 U.S., pp. 163, 176 (1965), and *Welsh v. United States*, 398 U.S., pp. 333, 344 (1970).
42. *United States v. MacIntosh*, 383 U.S., p. 605 (1931).
43. Ibid., pp. 633–634.
44. *United States v. Seeger*, 380 U.S., p. 163 (1965).
45. Ibid.
46. Ibid.
47. 398 U.S., pp. 333, 344 (1970).
48. 376 U.S., p. 255 (1964).
49. Ibid., p. 264.
50. Ibid., pp. 279–280.
51. Ibid., pp. 271–272.
52. Leo Pfeffer, The Supremacy of Free Exercise, *Georgetown Law Journal*, vol. 61, pp. 1115, 1122 (1973).
53. 430 U.S., p. 705 (1977).
54. Ibid.
55. Ibid., p. 716.
56. California Reports 2d, vol. 39, p. 121; Pacific Reporter 2d, vol. 245, p. 481 (1952).
57. Ibid., pp. 131–132; Pacific Reporter 2d, vol. 245, pp. 487–488 (citation omitted).

A First Look at Clergy Malpractice/Bergman

1. See, e.g., Gray, "The Insurer's Dilemma," *Industrial Law Journal*, vol. 51, p. 120 (1975).
2. The author recognizes that the term "clergyman" may be regarded as sexist. No such attitude is intended by him. In his own religious movement, wherein women are not yet ordained, he is an advocate of ordination for women.
3. M. Breecher, "Ministerial Malpractice," *Liberty*, March–April 1980, p. 15.
4. M. Breecher, "Ministerial Malpractice: Is It a Reasonable Fear?" *Trial*, July 1980, p. 11.

5. *Nally v. Grace Community Church of the Valley,* No. NCC-18668-B (Los Angeles County Superior Court, California, filed March 31, 1980).

6. In addition to clergy malpractice, the suit complains of wrongful death, negligence, and outrageous conduct.

7. See Notes and Comments, "Civil Liability for Causing or Failing to Prevent Suicide," *Loyola of Los Angeles Law Review,* vol. 12, p. 967 (1979).

8. U.S. Constitution Amendment I.

9. *McCulloch v. Maryland,* 17 U.S. (4 Wheat.), pp. 316, 431 (1819).

10. See *Engle v. Vitale,* 370 U.S., p. 421 at 437, n. 1 (1962), for a discussion of governmental aid to religion.

11. Thomas Jefferson, *Life and Selected Writings* (Modern Library, 1944), p. 332.

12. Joseph Story, *Two Commentaries on the Constitution of the United States* (5th ed., 1891), p. 632; see also *Walz v. Tax Commission of the City of New York,* 397 U.S., pp. 664, 676–677 (1970).

13. 330 U.S., p. 1 (1947).

14. Ibid., p. 19.

15. 343 U.S., p. 306 (1951).

16. *McCollum v. Board of Education of School District No. 71,* 333 U.S., p. 203 (1948).

17. 343 U.S., p. 325.

18. Ibid., p. 318.

19. See, e.g., *Serbian Eastern Orthodox Diocese for the United States of America and Canada v. Milivojevich,* 426 U.S., p. 696 (1976); *Presbyterian Church v. Mary Elizabeth Blue Hull Presbyterian Church,* 393 U.S., p. 440 (1969); *Kedroff v. St. Nicholas Cathedral,* 344 U.S., p. 94 (1952).

20. California Business and Professions Code, section 2063 (West Supp., 1981).

21. Ibid., section 4508 (West, 1974).

22. Ibid., section 17800.1 (West Supp., 1981).

23. Ibid., section 17804 (West Supp., 1981).

24. Ibid., section 17804(b) (West, 1964).

25. Ibid., section 17804(c) (West Supp., 1981).

26. I am indebted to my colleague Dr. Michael Menitoff for bringing this to my attention. He tells me further that, while never stated explicitly, the implicit understanding is that the amendment was specifically aimed at clergy who were entering private counseling practice.

27. California Business and Professions Code, section 17804(a) (West Supp., 1981).

28. California Administrative Code, vol. 16, pp. 1830, 1833.

29. California, Illinois, Minnesota, New York, and New Jersey.

30. *Malloy v. Fong,* California Reports 2d, vol. 37, pp. 356–366; Pacific Reporter 2d, vol. 232, pp. 241–247 (1951).

31. California Appellate Reports, 3d, vol. 90, p. 259; West's California Reporter, vol. 153, p. 322 (1979).

32. See also *Cantwell v. Connecticut,* 310 U.S., p. 296 (1940).

33. California Appellate Reports 3d, vol. 90, p. 275; West's California Reporter, vol. 153, p. 333. See also *Braunfeld v. Brown,* 366 U.S., p. 599 (1961); *Reynolds v. United States,* 98 U.S., p. 145 (1879).

34. See *Prince v. Commonwealth of Massachusetts,* 321 U.S., p. 158 (1944); *Theriault v. Carlson,* Federal Reporter 2d, vol. 495, p. 390 (5th Cir. 1974); *Church of Scientology of California v. Richardson,* Federal Reporter 2d, vol. 437, p. 214 (9th Cir. 1971); *United States v. Speers,* Federal Reporter 2d, vol. 443, p. 895 (5th Cir. 1971).

35. California Business and Professions Code, section 4508 (West, 1974 (emphasis added).

36. Federal Reporter 2d, vol. 495, p. 390 (5th Cir. 1974).

37. Ibid., p. 395.

38. Federal Reporter 2d, vol. 443, p. 895 (5th Cir. 1971).

39. *Prince v. Commonwealth of Massachusetts,* 321 U.S., p. 158 (1944).

40. Federal Supplement, vol. 278, p. 488 (1967).

41. *Church of Scientology of California v. Richardson,* Federal Reporter 2d, vol. 437, p. 214 (9th Cir. 1971).

42. 366 U.S., p. 420 (1961).

43. Ibid., p. 433.

44. Ibid., p. 436, but see pp. 571–581. Justice Douglas, in his dissenting opinion, while reiterating the religious origin, bases his dissent primarily on the lack of justification for mandatory closing in general and Sunday closing in particular as discriminatory against orthodox Jews and Sabbatarians.

45. Harvey M. Weinstein and Michael L. Russell, "Competency-Based Psychiatric Education," *American Journal of Psychiatry,* vol. 133 (August 1976), p. 935.

46. Henry B. Rothblatt and D. H. Leroy, "Avoiding Psychiatric Malpractice," *California Western Law Review,* vol. 9, p. 260 (1972); see also Gerald Corey, *Theory and Practice of Counseling and Psychotherapy* (Brooks/Cole Publishing Co., 1977), ch. 12.

47. See Babylonian Talmud, *Tractate Shabbath,* Folio 133b.

48. California Appellate Reports 2d, vol. 194, p. 282; West's California Reporter, vol. 15, p. 26 (1961). Fact and causation were uncontested; the only issue was the manner in which certain instructions were given to the jury.

49. Milton Malev, "Recognizing Possible Mental Illness" (unpublished material from a course on Pastoral Psychology at the Jewish Theological Seminary of America)

50. Rothblatt and Leroy, loc. cit., p. 260.

51. California Association of Marriage and Family Counselors, *Ethical Standards for CAMFC Counselors,* Section 3.5.

52. Corey, op. cit. note 46, pp. 213, 216.

53. Malev, op. cit. note 49.

54. See, e.g., California Evidence Code Sections 1030–1034; Illinois Annotated Statutes, ch. 51, section 48.1 (Smith-Hurd).

55. *Nally v. Grace Community Church of the Valley,* No. NCC-18668-B (Los Angeles County Superior Court, California, filed March 31, 1980).

56. *Valladao v. Firemen's Fund Indemnity Co.,* California Reports 2d, vol. 13, p. 322; Pacific Reporter 2d, vol. 89, p. 643 (1939).

57. Counsel for defendant Grace Community Church, in the Answer, filed June 13, 1980, argued:

"If 'spiritual counseling malpractice' is permitted, a foreseeable consequence might be the need for churches to post 'disclaimer' signs outside their pastors' offices, counseling rooms, or confessional booths warning the 'consumer' counselee/penitent of the 'subjective nature' of the 'cure.'

"The requisite warning might read: ATTENTION COUNSELEE (PENITENT).Due to potential lawsuits for spiritual malpractice, this counseling room (confessional booth) is no longer available to deal with anything other than clearly superficial problems. We suggest (but do not counsel) for your possible consideration the use of prayer and scripture, but you should do so at your own risk. If government-sponsored counseling services are unavailable due to lack of mental health funds, and you cannot afford private psychiatric care, a list of possible churches in this state who may be insured is available on request at the front office upon signing a Release from Referral Liability. If your problem is urgent and really serious, please be assured our prayers are with you. We wish you 'Godspeed' and hope you will visit when you are better.'"

3. Pastoral Accountability in the Bible and Theology/Southard

1. *Los Angeles Magazine,* November 1980, pp. 154ff.

2. The story is recorded with gusto by Robert Shaplen in *Free Love and Heavenly Sinners* (Alfred A. Knopf, 1954).

3. John L. McKenzie, *Authority and the Church* (Sheed & Ward, 1966), pp. 31–32.

4. This is the emphasis of a scholarly work on the church and ministry by Hans Küng, *The Church* (Doubleday & Co., 1976); see pp. 495–512.

5. See David Schuller, *Readiness for Ministry,* vol. 1, *Criteria* (Association for Theological Schools, 1975), pp. 6–77.

6. With these characteristics we have defined the pastorate as a profession as well as a calling. For definitions of the meaning of profes-

sional, see Talcott Parsons, *Essays in Sociological Theory*, rev. ed. (Free Press of Glencoe, 1964), pp. 34–49. For additional discussion of pastoral authority, see Bernard Cooke, *Ministry to Word and Sacrament* (Fortress Press, 1976), pp. 411ff.

7. Samuel Southard, *Pastoral Authority and Personal Relationships* (Abingdon Press, 1969), p. 57.

8. William Clebsch and Charles Jaekel, *Pastoral Care in Historical Perspective: An Essay with Exhibits* (Prentice-Hall, 1964).

9. Jay E. Adams, *Competent to Counsel* (Presbyterian & Reformed Publishing Co., 1970).

10. See, by John T. McNeill, *The Celtic Penitentials and Their Influence on Continental Christianity* (Paris, 1923), *Medieval Handbook of Penance* (Columbia University, 1938), and *A History of the Cure of Souls* (Harper & Brothers, 1951).

11. McNeill, *A History of the Cure of Souls*, pp. 319–330.

12. See *Issues Regarding Confidentiality of Data in the Cooperative Health Statistics Systems*, Department of Health, Education and Welfare, Publ. #80–1459 (1980); L. Everstine et al., "Privacy and Confidentiality in Psychotherapy," *American Psychologist*, vol. 35, no. 9 (September 1980), pp. 828–840; and G. Stanley Joslin, *The Minister's Law Handbook* (Channel Press, 1962), pp. 85, 115.

13. McNeill, *A History of the Cure of Souls*, p. 117.

14. The tradition of spiritual guidance has been traced and recommended for modern use by Kenneth Leech, *Soul Friend* (Harper & Row, 1977), and by Tilden Edwards, *Spiritual Friend* (Paulist Press, 1980).

15. McNeill, *A History of the Cure of Souls*, p. 148. For a general discussion of the church's dilemma with confession, see Clebsch and Jaekel, *Pastoral Care*, pp. 64–65.

16. McNeill, p. 176.

17. Ibid., p. 209.

18. Ibid., p. 226.

19. Ibid., p. 279.

20. See the December 1965 issue of *Pastoral Psychology*, especially the article by Liston O. Mills, "The Relationships of Discipline to Pastoral Care in Frontier Churches, 1800–1850: A Preliminary Study."

4. Church Discipline: Handle with Care/Southard

1. John T. McNeill, *A History of the Cure of Souls* (Harper & Brothers, 1951), pp. 324–327.

2. Ibid., p. 327.

3. Tilden Edwards, *Spiritual Friend* (Paulist Press, 1980), ch. 6.

4. The difficulties of maintaining this balance were demonstrated by Kenneth E. Kirk, an outstanding moral theologian of the 1920s, in

The Vision of God (London: Longmans, Green & Co., 1931). In a survey of early church practices, Bishop Kirk demonstrated the recurring problem of discipline as a tendency toward institutionalism, formalism (a code of rules), and rigorism (renunciation of the world).

5. This emphasis upon intervention and implied judgment was strongly resisted by early writers in the field of pastoral counseling. Seward Hiltner considered "a regular exposition of our views as pastor" as a move away from counseling (Seward Hiltner, *The Counselor in Counseling,* p. 136; Abingdon-Cokesbury Press, 1952). By the seventies, he had decided that "ethics" and "cure" ought not to be separated so categorically (Seward Hiltner, *Theological Dynamics,* p. 175; Abingdon Press, 1972).

6. It is unfortunate that *noutheteō,* which occurs about a dozen times in the New Testament, is magnified out of its context into a catchword for condemnation, as in the writings of Jay Adams (see Jay E. Adams, *Competent to Counsel,* p. xxi; Presbyterian & Reformed Publishing Co., 1970). A more biblical presentation would balance judgment and acceptance in the use of *noutheteō* and would give primary emphasis to the many usages of *parakaleō,* which is used over a hundred times in the New Testament.

7. Thomas C. Oden, *Pastoral Theology* (Harper & Row, 1983).

8. The background for this insistence was the Puritan movement in England, as described by E. S. Morgan, *The Visible Saints* (New York University Press, 1963), pp. 7ff. The struggle to establish these requirements for the clergy in the American colonies has been described by Leonard J. Trinterud, *The Forming of an American Tradition* (Westminster Press, 1949).

9. See Kenneth Leech, *Soul Friend* (Harper & Row, 1977).

10. William W. Sweet, "The Churches as Moral Courts of the Frontier," *Church History,* vol. 2, no. 1 (March 1933), p. 9.

11. See the quotation from John Calvin's *Institutes of the Christian Religion* in William A. Clebsch and Charles R. Jaekel, *Pastoral Care in Historical Perspective: An Essay with Exhibits* (Prentice-Hall, 1964), p. 57. Also see the rest of the discussion on reconciling, pp. 56–66.

12. Hannah Colm, "Healing as Participation," *Psychiatry,* vol. 16 (1953), pp. 99–111.

13. Joseph Sittler, "Acceptance, Human and Divine," *The Divinity School News* (University of Chicago), May 1, 1958, p. 4.

14. See Morgan, *Visible Saints,* p. 62.

15. For studies of the holiness emphasis, see Robert Mapes Anderson, *Vision of the Disinherited* (Oxford University Press, 1979); Russell Spittler, ed., *Perspectives on the New Pentecostalism* (Baker Book House, 1977); Donald Dayton, "The Holiness Churches: A Significant Ethical Tradition," *Christian Century,* February 26, 1973. The rise of "fundamentalism," which often referred to the Scofield Reference Bible as a text, may be studied in such books as James Barr's *Funda-*

mentalism (Westminster Press, 1978) and George M. Marsden's *Fundamentalism and American Culture* (Oxford University Press, 1980).

16. Morgan, *Visible Saints*, p. 26.

17. The practices of frontier Protestants have been surveyed by William W. Sweet, *The Baptist* (Henry Holt & Co., 1931) and *The Presbyterians: Religion on the American Frontier, 1783–1840* (Harper & Brothers, 1936); Charles Johnson, *The Frontier Camp Meeting* (Southern Methodist University Press, 1955); L. C. Rudolph, "Hoosier Zion" (Ph.D. dissertation, Yale University, 1958); W. B. Posey, *The Baptist Church in the Lower Mississippi Valley, 1776–1785* (University of Kentucky Press, 1957).

18. McNeill, *History of the Cure of Souls*, pp. 117ff.

19. Clebsch and Jaekel, *Pastoral Care in Historical Perspective*, pp. 253–262.

20. *Quarterly Review of the Methodist Episcopal Church South*, vol. 5 (April 1851), p. 282.

21. Kirk, *Vision of God*. The wide range of personal and social problems that came under discipline have been discussed by Cecil J. Cadouz, *The Early Church and the World* (Edinburgh: T. & T. Clark, 1925).

22. Morgan, *Visible Saints*, p. 51.

23. Oden, *Pastoral Theology*, p. 212.

5. Helping When the Risks Are Great/Needham

1. Jackson W. Carroll, Douglas W. Johnson, and Martin E. Marty, *Religion in America: 1950 to the Present* (Harper & Row, 1979), p. 104.

6. Confidentiality in the Pastoral Role/Malony

1. L. Everstine et al., "Privacy and Confidentiality in Psychotherapy," *American Psychologist*, vol. 35, no. 9 (1980), pp. 828–840.

2. H. Guervitz, "Tarasoff: Protective Privilege vs. Public Peril," *American Journal of Psychiatry*, vol. 134 (1977), pp. 289–292.

3. Everstine et al., loc. cit., p. 831.

4. Ibid., p. 829.

5. Ibid., pp. 829–830.

7. Insurance Protection for Church and Clergy/Needham

1. John F. Cleary, *Clergy Malpractice—The Insurance Carrier's Perspective* (Church Mutual Insurance Co., 1985), p. 3.

2. Yair Aharoni, *The No-Risk Society* (Chatham House Publishers, 1981), p. 1.

3. Ibid., pp. 49, 50.

4. Cleary, *Clergy Malpractice*, p. 4.

5. Ibid.

6. *Los Angeles Times,* September 14, 1985, section I, p. 28.

7. *The Church and the Legal Explosion* (Preferred Risk Mutual Insurance Company, 1985), p. 3.

8. Cleary, *Clergy Malpractice*, p. 7.

9. *The Church and the Legal Explosion,* p. 5.

10. Ibid., p. 3.

11. *Los Angeles Times,* September 14, 1985, section I, p. 28.

12. Ibid.

8. The Future of Ministry in a Changing World/Malony

1. Carnegie Samuel Calian, *Today's Pastor in Tomorrow's World,* rev. ed. (Westminster Press, 1982), pp. 21–36.

2. "Marian and the Elders," *Time,* March 26, 1984, p. 70.

3. Alastair W. Campbell, *Professional Care: Its Meaning and Practice* (Fortress Press, 1984), p. 5.

4. Paul Wilding, *Professional Power and Social Welfare* (Routledge & Kegan Paul, 1982).

5. Don S. Browning, *The Moral Context of Pastoral Care* (Westminster Press, 1983).

6. Theodore Runyon, ed., *Hope for the Church: Moltmann in Dialogue with Practical Theology* (Abingdon Press, 1979).

7. Paul Halmos, *The Faith of the Counsellors: A Study in the Theory and Practice of Social Case Work and Psychotherapy* (Schocken Books, 1966).

8. Daphne Statham, *Radicals in Social Work* (Routledge & Kegan Paul, 1978).

9. E. Brooks Holifield, *A History of Pastoral Care in America: From Salvation to Self-Realization* (Abingdon Press, 1983), p. 355.

10. James D. Whitehead and Evelyn E. Whitehead, *Method in Ministry: Theological Reflection and Christian Ministry* (Seabury Press, 1980), pp. 11–13.

11. Ibid., p. 13.

12. J. Gordon Melton and Robert L. Moore, *The Cult Experience: Responding to the New Religious Pluralism* (Pilgrim Press, 1982).

13. Margaret T. Singer, "Coming Out of the Cults," *Psychology Today,* vol. 12, no. 8 (1978), pp. 72–82.

Annotated Resources for Further Reading

Legal Issues in the Practice of Ministry by Lindell L. Gumper (Psychological Studies, 1981) presents a comprehensive overview of legal issues from the viewpoint of a therapist who is also an expert on legal accountability. As a consultant to clergy and religious organizations through Psychological Studies and Consultation Program, Inc., Dr. Gumper relates the interpretation of the law to the actual situation of a clergyperson who is in contact with the judicial process. The book is especially insightful concerning conduct in the courtroom (pp. 45–60).

Brief chapters summarize the major legal areas of interest to clergy: (1) negligence, which includes malpractice, (2) intentional harmful acts, and (3) contractual obligations.

Negligence is a problem that should cause clergy to look more deeply at such issues as the standard of care which is presumed to underlie pastoral practice and the standards that are appropriate to pastoral care and counsel. Dr. Gumper notes that clergy who direct their counsel toward the spiritual dimensions of a personal problem are less liable than clergy who define themselves as religious therapists and are indistinguishable from psychologists, social workers, and marriage and family counselors in their professional practice (pp. 18ff.).

Intentional harmful acts include libel and slander, invasion of privacy, and breach of confidentiality. The way in which a sermon mentions a person, family, or group can be a source of legal action. I suspect that in the rare instance of a suit against a pastor concerning counseling, the contributing cause may be demeaning statements against the plaintiff or the plaintiff's way of life and religion from the pulpit or in teaching sessions for church leaders. Wrongful commitment, as in the case of malicious lies about a person who may be sent to a mental hospital, would also be cause for suit. And there is always the touchy subject of undue influence, by which a pastor uses the aura of religious office to gain financial or sexual favors. Assault and battery charges are closely related to this.

Contractual obligations involve the usual expectations of faithfulness in a profession, both to meet a standard of care and to be available, alert, and responsible in the exercise of that care. Clergy often are guided by messianic fantasies to promise more than they can provide, such as "If you will covenant with me, I will save your marriage" or "No one who has sought my counsel has ever carried out the threat of suicide."

The insightful chapter on clergy in the courtroom includes knowing what to do when a subpoena comes, preparing for testimony, understanding the adversary attitude of attorneys, and staying cool during cross-examination.

Appendixes list laws on confidentiality by state and provide a sample authorization for release of counseling information to the courts.

The Right to Silence by William H. Tiemann and John C. Bush (Abingdon Press, 1983) is a welcome update of the original edition of 1964. The first edition may be described by the rare adjectives "prophetic" and "appropriate," for it contained well-documented evidence on the development of confidentiality from the common law of England into the free church experience of America and a discerning presentation of problems in 1964 concerning "clergy privilege." Its impact may be seen in the expansion of the brief statutes concerning confidentiality on the books of thirty-seven states at the time of the 1964 edition (Appendix II) to the amplified versions found on the books of forty-nine states in 1983.

As the title suggests, the principal concern is the right to silence, which is a more useful rubric than the medieval concern for the seal of the confessional. Who is to determine what is a confession in the modern pastoral counseling practice? This is one of the current questions posed by the authors. They have moved from historical analysis of the confessional to such pressing problems as the status of laypersons as counselors and privileged communication between members of a church staff concerning the personal problems of a parishioner An author and case index is included.

Malpractice: A Guide for Mental Health Professionals by Ronald Jay Cohen (Free Press, 1979) is of special interest to clergy who practice as marriage and family therapists, pastoral counselors, or pastoral psychotherapists. As the preceding texts by Gumper and Tiemann and Bush show, liability increases as pastors move beyond duties as spiritual directors into areas of competence that are not defined by their ecclesiastical associations. For these pastors, Cohen provides a comprehensive discussion of relevant cases with some specific advice on the avoidance of legal jeopardy. The landmark case of *Tarasoff v.*

Regents of California is presented in excerpt as an appendix. In this case, mental health professionals were held liable because they did not use their diagnostic skills to protect a female college student against the homicidal act of a jilted suitor. Since a number of pastoral counselors and psychotherapy practitioners emphasize "assessment" or psychiatric diagnosis, the case has immediate impact on their liability.

I hope this review of current representative works will stimulate others to develop related volumes on (1) the definition of "pastoral" in terms of practice and legal responsibility, (2) the consensus—if there is any—of denominations and associations of pastoral counselors and societies for the advancement of pastoral theology concerning the standard of care that may reasonably be expected from any clergy in pastoral practice, and (3) the role and responsibilities of lay care-givers in relation to the definition of pastoral, the standard of care for clergy, and any legal liabilities.

A related topic that will surface through these discussions is a broad treatment of "professional ethics." What standards are expected as a pastor discusses a client with a church staff member or a lay care-giver, or makes a referral to a psychiatrist, or accepts a referral from a mental health professional? What about the wide-ranging impact of the respect—or lack of it—that pastors show to each other, to staff, to church members, and to persons of other professions? This will involve discussion on character and the cardinal virtues and may mitigate the current professional competitiveness, manipulation, and status-seeking that is seldom addressed in literature on the pastor as person and professional.

SAMUEL SOUTHARD

Contributors

Ben Zion Bergman, J.D., is an attorney and rabbi who is dean of students and senior lecturer in rabbinic literature at the University of Judaism in Los Angeles, California.

Samuel E. Ericsson, LL.B., formerly director of the Center for Law and Religious Freedom, is presently executive director of the Christian Legal Society in Washington, D.C. He represented Grace Community Church in the Nally litigation.

H. Newton Malony, Ph.D., is a clinical psychologist and United Methodist minister who is professor and director of programs in the integration of psychology and theology in the Graduate School of Psychology, Fuller Theological Seminary, Pasadena, California.

Thomas L. Needham, Ed.D., is a marriage counselor and Baptist minister in Encino, California. He is director of the Needham Institute and adjunct professor at Azusa Pacific University.

Samuel Southard, Ph.D., is a pastoral counselor and Southern Baptist minister who is professor of pastoral theology in the School of Theology of Fuller Theological Seminary.